7.

July 11, 2016

Dr. MINH LAM

God's Miracles

His Faith, and His Escape from Vietnam by Boat

Photograph of the refugee boat holding forty-seven Vietnamese refugees, taken on the Pacific Ocean on October 5, 1980, 165 miles from the Vietnamese coast. The author is the second from the left.

REVEREND DR. MINH VAN LAM

In loving memory of my beloved wife, Khanh Minh Lam.

Photograph of the Vietnamese refugees from the boat rescue, taken October 1980 at the Baptist chapel in the Leamsing Refugee Camp in Thailand.

Photograph of the American merchant vessel, Leslie Lykes, which rescued the 47 Vietnamese refugees.

Praise for *God's Miracles*

Would you like to discover a deeper and mature life in Christ? Do you know that a life with a purpose is a life of a grateful and faithful attitude that can change your world? This unique book will not only help you become a true disciple of Christ, but also allow you to experience God in a spiritual journey. *God's Miracles*, by Dr. Minh Van Lam, will help you discover a number of great miraculous stories through God's grace, develop spiritual maturity through trials, seek peace through God's love, and gain the power of wisdom through Biblical principles.
  Rev. Dr. Tan Viet Ngo, Vice President of Vietnamese Baptist Theological School; Author of *Purpose-Driven Spiritual Life*, Canada

I have been touched by the book *God's Miracles*, written by Dr. Minh Van Lam. The book retells of how our Lord Jesus Christ still works and has performed His miracles through the ages. As the nephew of Dr. Lam, I was close with him during my childhood and youth. My sister was with his family in the same refugee boat and experienced the amazing rescue. For these reasons, I believe what he has retold in his book is a true account of what happened.
  Rev. Dr. Quang Minh Ngo, President of the Vietnamese Evangelical Church, Australia

God's miracles are still working in the lives of Christ's believers today. God's greatest miracle is His salvation for all of us. 2 Corinthians 5:17 recorded, "If anyone is in Christ, the new creation has come: The old has gone, the new is here!" (NIV). In the book of God's Miracles, Dr. Minh Lam carefully explained how God's miracles working in the lives of His people in the Bible then and testified God's love, faithfulness, and protection upon his family members during the Vietnam War and till this day. Many stories of his family's journey inspired us to deepen our relationship with God daily. This book tells us how God's amazing grace working in the lives of His beloved people. The purpose of this book is to glorify God and to encourage everyone to trust in Him and be faithful to Him till the Day of Jesus Christ's return.

    Rev. Dr. Peter Hong Le, D. Min., Director of Vietnamese Mission Board; Senior Pastor of the Vietnamese Faith Baptist Church, Dallas, Texas

Author's Note

His Will
The Bible recorded the miracles performed according to God's will. The book of Genesis describes the creation of the universe, the earth, the human being among nature, the birds in the sky, the fish in the water, and the animals on earth. His will consists of

a. His own plan for eternity, natural activities, and blessings from God—"He predestined us to adoption as sons through Jesus Christ to Himself, according to the kind intention of His will, to the praise of the glory of His grace, which He freely bestowed on us in the Beloved" (Ephesians 1:5–6)—and
b. the prayers of His children, which match His will for His plan according to the situation of one period of time, such as Hannah's prayer and King Hezekiah's supplication.

His Compassion
God's miracles are performed for His compassion, such as the widow's only son's funeral in Nain. His miracle with compassion caused the boy to rise from the dead.

His Penalty
God's miracles are performed for His penalty. For example, the flood during Noah's time killed everyone on earth except Noah's family.

He Does
God's performs His miracles Himself; this means He does the miracles—not any other spirits or mankind. He made the different languages in the world so that the construction of the Tower of Babel would not be completed as desired.

The Angels Do
God's miracles are performed through the angels, who received His order according to His desires. An angel announced the good news to the shepherds on the night the Lord Jesus Christ was born in Bethlehem.

His Servants Do
Servants like Moses, the prophet Elisha, Peter, and Paul sometimes perform God's miracles.

How to See God's Miracles

1. Pray with faith. (See Matthew 17:19–21.)
2. Ask for forgiveness. (See 1 John 1:9.)
3. Promise to be grateful. (See 1 Samuel 1:11.)
4. Wait for the answers. (See Luke 2:25–32.)
5. Serve the Lord after receiving God's miracles. (See Luke 8:1–3.)

Contents

Author's Note xi
Acknowledgments xvii
Preface xix

I. What I Know about God's Miracles 1

Chapter 1   I Am Interested in the Miracle 3
Chapter 2   Miracle Performance 10
Chapter 3   Miracle in God's Will 26
Chapter 4   Miracle for God's Compassion 37
Chapter 5   Miracle for God's Penalty 49

II. God's Miracles for My Civilian Life 59

Chapter 1   The First Miracle: No More Poverty 61
Chapter 2   Some Extraordinary Happenings 68
Chapter 3   The Second Miracle: What a Strange Birth 83
Chapter 4   The Third Miracle: Missed a Bomb Explosion 88

III. God's Miracles for My Military Service 93

Chapter 1   The Fourth Miracle: God's Response to My Prayer 95

Chapter 2   The Fifth Miracle: Missed Another Bomb
            Explosion 109
Chapter 3   What a Strange Disease 111
Chapter 4   The Sixth Miracle: An Overseas Training 114
Chapter 5   The Seventh Miracle: A Miraculous Discharge .. 118

IV.   God's Miracles for My Christian Life 125

Chapter 1   Two More Children 127
Chapter 2   A Helpful Presentation 133
Chapter 3   The Eighth Miracle:
            My Canoe Was Not Caught 137
Chapter 4   The Visions for the Flight 138
Chapter 5   The Ninth Miracle: Boat Rescue 144

V.   My Thanksgiving for God's Miracles 153

Chapter 1   Mission in the Refugee Camps 155
Chapter 2   Christian Ministry in the United States 164
Chapter 3   The Tenth Miracle:
            Christian Educational Improvement 175
Chapter 4   My Thanksgiving for God's Miracles 190

VI.   Misunderstanding of God's Miracles..................... 195

Chapter 1   God Still Performs Miracles 197
Chapter 2   Don't Force God to Perform Miracles 202

God's Miracles in the Bible 205

Acknowledgments

Thanks to the Lord's help, by His miracles, the dangerous trip from Vietnam to Thailand became a very quick, safe, and interesting journey for me—like a fun cruise. It took the tiny, old wooden boat carrying forty-seven refugees less than two days—from 7:00 p.m. on October 3, 1980, to 5:00 p.m. on October 5, 1980—to reach the *Leslie Lykes*, an American merchant vessel. According to the ship's captain, the vessel was located on the Pacific Ocean 165 miles from the Vietnamese coast. We praised the Lord for His compassion (see Psalm 107:23–30), and we have not forgotten our American benefactors: the ship's captain, first mate Blaine Buckley, and all the sailors and passengers of that ship.

Many American Christians of the Grand Ave Baptist Church of Fort Smith, Arkansas; First Baptist Church of Pensacola, Florida; and other American churches in Orlando, Florida, where I gave my testimony of the boat trip on the Pacific Ocean, encouraged and reminded me to write this book. I would like to express my deep gratitude to these beloved brothers and sisters in Christ for their genuine love.

I have not forgotten Rev. Truong, my dear partner of the program *Alpha and Omega*, which has been broadcasted on Vietnam Public Radio since 1997. I am grateful that he continuously encouraged me to write a book about my boat rescue.

I thank my dear children for their financial support, and especially for persuading me to write a book of our family's experience fleeing Vietnam in 1980. Thanks to my youngest daughter, Linh Thuy Lam, for her help in reviewing the book in an editorial capacity and overseeing my book projects.

My appreciation should be expressed to Rev. Ho, who played an important role in making this book look better. I am always thankful to Dr. Whitten, the executive director of NorthStar Church Network, for helping a great deal in the completion of the book. In addition, I am grateful to Ms. Luckett as the book editor. I sincerely express my heartfelt thanks to the publisher for all their efforts to make this book available.

May the Lord Jesus Christ bless you all for your encouragement, assistance, and promotion.

Hallelujah! Praise the Lord. Amen!

Preface

I have given my testimony at several American churches since I arrived in the United States in 1981. The first American church was the Grand Avenue Baptist Church in Fort Smith, Arkansas, where I was called to be the first mission pastor of the Vietnamese congregation by Rev. Jim Files, in charge of the Vietnamese congregation, and Dr. Moore, the senior pastor, in 1982.

My testimony is about how the Lord miraculously transformed me from an unhealthy and uneducated boy into a schoolteacher and a soldier and ultimately took me out of the military service. It is also about how the Lord set me free from the reeducation camps, and especially about the boat rescue, in which a tiny, old wooden boat carried forty-seven refugees to the *Leslie Lykes*, an American merchant vessel on the Pacific Ocean 165 miles from the Vietnamese coast. We all were brought to the United States as refugees, thanks to the generosity of the US government and Americans, who largely opened their arms to welcome us.

After sharing my testimony, many American Christians in the United States encouraged me to write a book about the boat rescue. I said yes, but the book was not actually completed until the year 2014, when I heard God's call: "Minh, write about God's miracles for your personal life with blessings." Since my first ministries in the United States, I have preached of God's miracles in many sermons. However, this was not enough; the Lord wanted me to write.

I now write this book: (1) as a testimony about God's miracles in response to Christian prayer; (2) as a memoir of a dangerous trip on the Pacific Ocean for my children and grandchildren to read in order to praise the Lord; (3) as an expression of appreciation to my benefactors, the ship's captain, my dear brother, Blaine Buckley, and my dear sister, D. Anne Buckley; (4) as evangelism and an invitation for those who trust in the Lord and accept Him as their personal Savior; and (5) to raise awareness of a need for financial support in order to build a simple house in Saigon, South Vietnam, that will serve as a church for the blind.

The book indicates what I lived, saw, heard, felt, thought, and experienced. Nothing was an illusion. I did, however, experience visions from God to encourage me during the Pacific Ocean crossing. This is similar to the biblical dreams in which Joseph dreamed of his bright future; Joseph, Mary's husband, dreamed of Mary's immaculate conception; and Pharaoh dreamed of seven sleek and fat cows eaten by seven ugly and gaunt cows. I am just a little common man who used to be poor and unhealthy, but I received many blessings from God through His miracles. I believe God's miracles may happen to you, too!

This book is not perfect in some aspects. It really needs your opinion and feedback as a precious contributor to the book's value; this will allow me to create a better revised edition. I sincerely appreciate your comments and help to better this book so that it might become a close companion to everyone in the future.

May the Lord Jesus Christ bless you,
Minh Van Lam

Section I

What I Know about God's Miracles

Chapter 1

I Am Interested in the Miracle

Since my boyhood, sitting on the front bench in the church, I attentively listened to the preacher's sermons. I was very interested in God's works among His children, God's mercy to the sinners, God's compassion to the poor, and God's miracles in response to prayers. I especially loved to hear about God's miracles, because I really needed them.

I looked in several dictionaries to see the definitions of the term "miracle." Many definitions did not satisfy me, because God was not mentioned in them. I like any definition of the word "miracle" that includes the phrase "by God's supernatural performance." A "miracle" without God's action, is not really a miracle but just a human action. It is not an extraordinary, outstanding, or unusual action.

Nature shows God's works, and God's works are performed through His miracles. When God did something in the past that has been recorded in the Bible, He did so through miracles. The universe, the earth, human beings, and animals were created by God's miracles. Genesis, the first book of the Bible, describes creation with a single sentence: "Then God said, 'Let there be light,' and there was light" (Genesis 1:3).

We can say that God's works are God's miracles, and God's miracles are God's works, because God's works are more difficult than man's works, and man cannot do God's works. Man's works are not miracles; and man cannot perform miracles if God does not allow man to do so. However, God can perform miracles through man's hands.

The whole Bible is the holy book full of God's miracles. What are God's miracles for? To let the reader know God's power, which can accomplish any difficult thing and can solve any problem, as these statements prove:

1. "Is anything too difficult for the LORD?" (Genesis 18:14a)
2. "'Not by might nor by power, but by My Spirit', says the LORD of hosts." (Zechariah 4:6)
3. "The things that are impossible with people are possible with God." (Luke 18:27)

The professional fishermen went to the Sea of Galilee for fishing, "and that night they caught nothing" (John 21:3). The Lord Jesus came and told them, "Cast the net on the right-hand side of the boat and you will find a catch" (John 21:6). They did what He said, and they "drew the net to land, full of large fish, a hundred and fifty-three" (John 21:11).

This was just one little action out of the billions of great things that God has done for mankind around the world from creation to modern times, but man actually ignores these moments, instead relying on his own ability and strength. That is why they failed, lamented, wept, and felt depressed and frustrated.

This is the reason an aging man, having previously experienced sickness, poverty, tragedy, imprisonment, separation, isolation, danger, and God's involvement through supernatural miracles, wrote this book. I am so happy to tell you what I know about God's miracles in this book of my personal life stories so that you might use these examples if you ever encounter something similar. My prayer is that you can continue following the Lord Jesus Christ, relying on only Him in everything.

Before sharing my life stories, full of God's miracles, I would like to share some examples of some great and important events recorded in the Bible: the creation of the universe, earth, and mankind; the great flood during Noah's time; the Tower of Babel's destruction; Israel's crossing of the Red Sea; the collapse of Jericho; the sun standing still and the moon stopping (see Joshua 10:13); and the blind receiving sight, the lame walking, the lepers being cleansed, the deaf hearing, and the dead being raised up (see Luke 7:22).

I believe God's will is for His miracles to show His power, grace, mercy, compassion, plan, teaching, and even penalty and destruction. Reading the Bible, I realize that the Lord loves the world (see John 3:16), and "love is from God" and "God is love" (1 John 4:7–8). The Lord Jesus Christ had never refused anyone's request, even those who were Gentiles and therefore not considered His people. He had healed a Roman centurion's servant, who was lying paralyzed at home, fearfully tormented in Capernaum. The Lord immediately said to him, "I will come and heal him" (Matthew 8:7). He did not hesitate; He never said, "Let me think," or "Let me go tomorrow," or "Is he an Israelite?" or "I need to finish my job here first. Then I will go to see your servant."

When Lazarus, His close friend, got seriously sick, He did not go to see him right away after Martha and Mary sent word to Him. Instead "He then stayed two days longer in the place where He was" (John 11:6), saying, "This sickness is not to end in death, but for the glory of God, so that the Son of God may be glorified by it" (John 11:4). He seemed to hesitate, but why? Both Martha and Mary made the same statement in reaction to this hesitation:

"Lord, if You had been here, my brother would not have died" (John 11:21, 32).

Based on His statement in John 11:4, we know the following:

1. Lazarus would not die: "This sickness is not to end in death" (John 11:4).
2. The reason He did not move to see Lazarus right away was "for the glory of God, so that the Son of God may be glorified by it." Lazarus' death was for God's glory; it was like a man blind from birth "so that the works of God might be displayed in him" (John 9:1–3).

Both Lazarus's death and the man blind from birth were healed for God's glory because the Lord Jesus Christ used these situations to demonstrate His powerful works in order to be ready for His coming to Jerusalem and the warm welcome from the crowd who took the branches of the palm trees and shouted, "Hosanna! BLESSED IS HE WHO COMES IN THE NAME OF THE LORD, even the King of Israel" (John 12:13).

The Gospel of Mark, in only the first chapter, describes the Lord's urgent works with the use of adverbs like "immediately." (See Mark 1:10, 12, 18, 21, 29, 30.)

> Now after John had been taken into custody, Jesus came into Galilee, preaching the gospel of God ... As He was going along by the Sea of Galilee ... and immediately on the Sabbath He entered the synagogue ... and immediately after they came out of the synagogue, they came into the house of Simon and Andrew, with James and John ... When evening came, after the sun had set, they began bringing to Him all who were ill and those who were demon-possessed. ... In the early morning, while it was still

dark, Jesus got up, left the house, and went away to a scheduled place, and was praying there ... He said to them, "Let us go somewhere else to the towns nearby, so that I may preach there also; for that is what I came for." (Mark 1:14–38)

The Lord Jesus Christ, during His earthly ministry, performed many miracles to heal "many who were ill with various diseases, and cast out many demons" (Mark 1:34a). His wonderful miracles attracted crowds, as mentioned in Scripture: "And they were coming to Him from everywhere" (Mark 1:45). "Jesus withdrew to the sea with His disciples; and a great multitude from Galilee followed; and also from Judea, and from Jerusalem, and from Idumea, and beyond the Jordan, and the vicinity of Tyre and Sidon, a great number of people heard of all that He was doing and came to Him" (Mark 3:7–8).

Anyone who saw His miracles was greatly surprised, because no one from ancient times, not even the priests, prophets, or the great people in Scripture—like Moses, Abraham, Samuel, or Daniel—could do such things. They admired Him. Some trusted in Him; became His disciples; and others followed Him for only a little while. However, some hated and opposed Him. They were the Jewish leaders, who were afraid that His good reputation would influence a whole nation to follow Him: "What are we doing? For this man is performing many signs. If we let Him go on like this, all men will believe in Him, and the Romans will come and take away both our place and our nation" (John 11:47b–48).

They finally found a way to destroy Him—by delivering Him to the Roman Empire for crucifixion. And their plan was successful: the Lord Jesus Christ died on the cross, as they desired.

At least they thought their plan put an end to the Lord's miracles; but, unfortunately for them, on the third day, news of the Lord's resurrection spread around Jerusalem. They then used money to lie to people about His disciples, saying they stole the Lord's dead body.

If the Jewish priests and the Pharisees were alive today, they would feel ashamed because the church now observes the Lord's resurrection—which provides a different view of God's miracles, in my mind.

My point is that the whole Bible is full of God's miracles—true stories of His actual works, not legends. God's miracles belong to God, not mankind. They show God is omnipresent, not just in heaven. God is omnipotent, not to be compared to the strength of the wind, the massiveness of the Pacific Ocean, the height of Mount Everest, or the vastness of the universe. God is omniscient but is nothing like our smartest scientists, scholars, philosophers, religious founders, or the spirit of mankind.

The Lord God is everywhere, knows everything, and can do anything. He performed miracles in ancient times, does so in this modern time, and will do so forever. "Jesus Christ is the same yesterday and today and forever" (Hebrews 13:8).

These are the reasons I have such interest in God's miracles:

1. I was born into a poor family but prayed that God's miracles would change my parents' poverty. And indeed, God did change the situation.
2. I was born in an unhealthy body but prayed that God's miracles would change my health. And indeed, God did change my health.

Those are just two things. There were many other problems in my life. I prayed to God, and He answered me with the miracles that are presented in this book. I hope you enjoy and tell others of this book in order that many people may know that God's miracles came to me, just as they can also come to others.

However, I do not think everyone in the world is interested in these miracles; many people, including atheists, still doubt the existence of miracles. To them the Bible is just a book full of legends—imaginative stories created by human beings who intended to bring the readers' minds to a fairy-tale land of illusions.

This purpose of this book is not to argue with those who doubt the existence of miracles. If you were not interested in miracles, you would have never been attracted to the title "God's Miracles" on the front cover of this book. This kind of book would never be placed on your bookshelf if you didn't believe. Continue reading and you will continue to believe. All the stories contained within these pages are true accounts from my life. My purpose in telling them to you is to praise the Lord for saving my life, my family, and the people from the boat, who are now living well in the United States and Europe.

Chapter 2

Miracle Performance

Miracles Performed by His Word

In the Creation
According to the Bible, God was the Creator: "In the beginning God created the heavens and the earth" (Genesis 1:1). The Creator consists of three persons: "Then God said, 'Let Us make man in Our image, according to Our likeness'" (Genesis 1:26a). The Holy Spirit is one person: "The Spirit of God was moving over the surface of the waters." (Genesis 1:2b). The Lord Jesus Christ is one person: "For by Him all things were created, both in the heavens and on earth, visible and invisible, whether thrones or dominions or rulers or authorities—all things have been created through Him and for Him" (Colossians 1:16). God created the universe, the sun, moon, stars, earth, animals, trees, oceans, rivers, and the mountains by His word: "Then God said, 'Let there be light'; and there was light" (Genesis 1:3).

In the World's Languages: The people of the world said, "Come, let us build for ourselves a city, and a tower whose top will reach into heaven, and let us make for ourselves a name, otherwise we will be scattered abroad over the face of the whole earth" (Genesis

11:4). Seeing their city, God said, "Come, let Us go down and there confuse their language, so that they will not understand one another's speech" (Genesis 11:7). All of the languages in the world were created by the Lord's word.

In the Wind and the Sea: Chapter 4 of Mark explains that the Lord Jesus Christ went with His twelve disciples to the other side of the sea in a boat at evening. While the Lord was asleep on the cushion at the stern, "there arose a fierce gale of wind, and the waves were breaking over the boat" (Mark 4:37). His disciples were so frightened that "they woke Him up and said to Him, 'Teacher, do You not care that we are perishing?' And He got up, rebuked the wind and said to the sea, 'Hush, be still.' And the wind died down and it became perfectly calm" (Mark 4:38b–39).

In the Resurrection

1. **Lazarus of Bethany**: Lazarus of Bethany was the brother of Martha and Mary, and also the close friend of the Lord Jesus Christ. There came a time when he was seriously sick, and the Lord Jesus was informed, but He did not come to see him until his death. When the Lord came to his house, Martha said, "Lord, by this time there will be a stench, for he has been dead four days" (John 11:39). The Lord came with them to Lazarus's tomb, and then He prayed, and He cried out with a loud voice, "Lazarus, come forth" (John 11:43). Lazarus, who was once dead, walked out of the tomb, having been resurrected.

2. **A Young Man of Nain**: When the Lord Jesus Christ approached the city gate of Nain, a dead man was being carried out to the cemetery for burial. He was a young man, the only son of a widow. The Lord saw her weep.

"He felt compassion for her, and said to her, 'Do not weep.' And He came up and touched the coffin" and said "'Young man, I say to you, arise!'" That young man, once dead, sat up and spoke. The Lord Jesus gave him back to the widow, his mother. (See Luke 7:11–15.)

3. **Jairus's Daughter:** Jairus was an official of the synagogue. His only daughter, who was about twelve years old, was seriously ill and dying. He came and fell at the Lord Jesus Christ's feet to ask Him to come to his house and heal his dear daughter. While Jairus was trying to speak with Christ, the Lord met a woman who had suffered from a hemorrhage for twelve years. She "came up behind Him and touched the fringe of His cloak, and immediately her hemorrhage stopped" (Luke 8:44). He took time to ask a question and talked to her, saying afterward, "Daughter, your faith has made you well; go in peace" (Luke 8:48). While He was busy with the woman, someone from Jairus's home came and said, "Your daughter has died; do not trouble the Teacher anymore." The Lord came to his house anyway and stepped into the child's room with His disciples Peter, James, and John, saying, "Child, arise!" Her spirit returned and she was resurrected. The Lord told the family to let her eat. (See Luke 8:41–56.)

4. **In the Rapture:** In the first letter to the church of Thessalonians, the apostle Paul mentioned that in the rapture the church would be caught up by these words: "For the Lord Himself will descend from heaven with a shout, with the voice of the archangel and with the trumpet of God, and the dead in Christ will rise first. Then we who are alive and remain will be caught up together with them in the clouds to meet the Lord in

the air, and so we shall always be with the Lord" (1 Thessalonians 4:16–18). A "shout" is a direct call from the Lord's mouth for the dead to rise, like the Lord Jesus' shout for Lazarus to rise.

5. **In Making All Things New**: After ruling over the world for one thousand years of peace, the Lord will release Satan, who will deceive people for fighting against the Lord. Satan will be defeated and be thrown into the lake of fire forever. Then the Lord will sit upon the great white throne and judge all of mankind from creation to the end of the age. A guilty verdict will result in this: "If anyone's name was not found written in the book of life, he was thrown into the lake of fire" (Revelation 20:15).

The Lord who sits on the throne will say, *"Behold, I am making all things new."* (Revelation 21:5) You will see "a new heaven and a new earth; for the first heaven and the first earth passed away, and there is no longer any sea ... a loud voice from the throne, saying, 'Behold, the Tabernacle of God is among men, and He will dwell among them, and they shall be His people, and God Himself will be among them, and He will wipe away every tear from their eyes; and there will no longer be any death; there will no longer be any mourning, or crying, or pain; the first things have passed away'" (Revelation 21:1–4).

Miracles Performed through Angels

The book of Hebrews records the creation of the angels: "And of the angels He says, 'WHO MAKES HIS ANGELS WINDS, AND HIS MINISTERS A FLAME OF FIRE'" (Hebrews 1:7);

with their works, "Are they not all ministering spirits, sent out to render service for the sake of those who will inherit salvation?" (Hebrews 1:14).

Those two verses show the origin and the role of the angels, who were the original creatures and servants of God. The Lord God made the angels to use for His works and serve the Lord by helping man. For instance, the Lord wanted to destroy the cities of Sodom and Gomorrah as described, "And the LORD said, 'The outcry of Sodom and Gomorrah is indeed great, and their sin is exceedingly grave. I will go down now, and see if they have done entirely according to its outcry, which has come to Me; and if not, I will know'" (Genesis 18:20–21). The Lord God commanded the angels to take Lot and his family out of the city to escape the burning fire. Lot hesitated; therefore, the angels "seized his hand and the hand of his wife and the hands of his two daughters, for the compassion of the LORD was upon him; and they brought him out, and put him outside the city" (Genesis 19:16).

So when reading the Bible, if you read a passage in which a miracle happened, you should know for sure who performed that miracle: God Himself, an angel, or man.

Now let's explore a few more examples of God using angels to perform His miracles.

The term "the angel" appears often in the Bible, both in the Old Testament and the New Testament. The first book of the Pentateuch, also known as the Five Books of Moses, is Genesis. This book records the creation of the universe and the world—the first events in the universe and on the earth. The book presents the angels' appearances on various occasions to help people according to the Lord's command.

Sarai harshly treated Hagar, an Egyptian woman and Abraham's second wife, because "her mistress was despised in her sight." (Genesis 16:4) She fled from Sarai and wandered in the wilderness near a spring of water, where the angel of the Lord met her to encourage her and told her to come back to her mistress's house, saying to her, "Behold, you are with child, And you will bear a son; And you shall call his name Ishmael, Because the Lord has given heed to your affliction" (Genesis 16:11). The angel of the Lord was sent to Hagar to command her return and tell her of her son's future.

The angels appeared to Lot, Abraham's nephew in Sodom, purposely to save his whole family from the destruction of the sinning city by "brimstone and fire from the Lord out of heaven" (Genesis 19:23). Sometimes the Bible simply refers to them as "the angels," such as "Now the two angels came to Sodom in the evening" (Genesis 19:1), and "When morning dawned, the angels urged Lot" (Genesis 19:15). But sometimes the Bible also refers to them as "the men" (Genesis 19:10) and "the two men" (Genesis 19:12).

There are some special things to note about these two angels. First, they looked like men. Second, they were handsome. The "men of the city, the men of Sodom, surrounded the house, both young and old, all the people from every quarter, and they called to Lot and said to him, 'Where are the men who came to you tonight? Bring them out to us that we may have relations with them'" (Genesis 19:4–5). Third, the Lord sent them to destroy the city. Fourth, the angels performed a miracle: "They struck the men who were at the doorway of the house with blindness" (Genesis 19:11). And finally, fifth, they took Lot, his wife, and his two daughters out of Sodom and told them not to look behind them or stay anywhere in the city. (See Genesis 19:17.) Their mission was successfully completed when Lot, with his two daughters, hurried to the small city named Zoar. (See Genesis 19:22.)

The prophet Elijah killed many Baal prophets of Queen Jezebel. The queen was so angry she threatened to kill Elijah, who ran to the wilderness and stayed under a juniper tree. An angel came, touched him, and told him to eat. Elijah saw a bread cake and a jar of water. After his meal, he lay down again. The angel patiently came to him a second time and said to him, "Arise, eat, because the journey is too great for you" (1 Kings 19:7). He rose to eat and drink, and then it took him forty days and nights to arrive at Mount Horeb, where he heard God talk to him (1 Kings 19:1–9).

The angel was definitely sent to comfort and encourage the prophet during this stressful and frustrating time. In addition to miracles, angels can bless the spirit with encouragement, comfort, and counseling.

Miracles Performed through Man

The Bible says the Lord allowed man to perform miracles. Miracles were performed by spiritual and Godly men, either prophets in the Old Testament or the Lord Jesus Christ's disciples and apostles in the New Testament. Only a few men performed miracles in both the Old Testament and the New Testament.

Some stories recorded in the Bible seem to be miracles, but actually they are just common stories, such as Jacob's story of the flocks with stripes, speckles, and spots, which explains the method of producing such animals: "Whenever the stronger of the flock were mating, Jacob would place the rods in the sight of the flock in the gutters, so that they might mate by the rods; but when the flock was feeble, he did not put them in; so the feebler were Laban's and the stronger Jacob's" (Genesis 30:41–42).

There were some great men in the Bible that never performed miracles but performed some strange and wonderful deeds that looked like miracles. However, they were simply using their talents and gifts the Lord gave them: (1) Joseph, in the book of Genesis, interpreted dreams; (2) Samson, in the book of Judges, killed a thousand Philistines with just the jawbone of a donkey; (3) David, in the book of 1 Samuel, struck Goliath, the Philistine champion, and killed him; (4) three friends of Daniel in the book of Daniel were put in the fire, which "had no effect on the bodies of these men nor was the hair of their head singed, nor were their trousers damaged, nor had the smell of fire even come upon them" (Daniel 3:27); (5) Daniel was put into the lions' den and was saved by God's angel, who "shut the lions' mouths" (Daniel 6:22); (6) Peter, in the book of Acts, was put in prison, which four squads of soldiers guarded, and an angel came to set him free; and (7) Paul, also in the book of Acts, was caught and brought by boat to Rome, but when the ship arrived at the island called Malta, it sank, and the soldiers planned to kill the prisoners, but "the centurion wanting to bring Paul safely through, kept them from their intention" (Acts 27:43). During Paul's stay on Malta, "a viper came out because of the heat and fastened itself on his hand"(Acts 28:3). Everyone thought he would die, but he was safe.

Just a few men with God's power and approval could perform these miracles. In spite of the miracles these men performed, the Bible reader should realize their human personalities and weaknesses.

Miracles Performed through Moses

The Lord called Moses from the midst of the bush to give him a mission. He hesitated and gave an excuse for his refusal: "Who am I, that I should go to Pharaoh, and that I should bring the sons of Israel out of Egypt?… What if they will not believe me or listen to what I say? For they may say, 'The Lord has not appeared to you!'" (Exodus 3:11, 4:1). Moses was right to say so, because it was hard for people to trust a man like him. He did not have any special talents—not even skills of speech. He was just a reluctant prince and a shepherd.

But God has a way to transform a human spirit into a godly servant of the Lord. He had a way to transform Moses, so as Moses would not refuse. He asked Moses, "What is that in your hand?" (Exodus 4:2). A staff was in Moses' hand. It was not a gun, a sword, a spear, or any kind of weapon, but the simple staff of a shepherd. It was not powerful or able to perform miracles. He commanded Moses, "Throw it on the ground" (Exodus 4:3). Moses obeyed; his staff became a serpent that made him fearful and caused him to run away. When it was still in his hand, the staff was his friend—very useful for him in some aspects. But when he dropped it, it became a wild animal—very poisonous and dangerous. What did Moses think? He preferred to keep the staff in his hand. If he did not take it back up, he would have regret. He waited for God's next command: "Stretch out your hand and grasp it by its tail" (Exodus: 4:4). He obeyed; the serpent became his staff once again.

What lessons did he take away from this encounter with the Lord?

1. Obedience is powerful.
2. Continue to hold the mission God gave.
3. Courage brings success.
4. God's power can accomplish anything.
5. God can change evil things into spiritual ones.

Reading the passage about the miracle of Moses' staff turning into a serpent and back into a staff again tells the Bible reader one precious thing: God can transform a normal human being into God's servant—one who can do great things through God's command and will. It is a supernatural miracle of love, mercy, and grace.

Man sinned against God, but "God is love" (1 John 4:8). And He did not avenge; rather, he saved man from eternal death through His only begotten Son's sacrifice on the cross (1 John 4:9–10).

Moses performed a lot of miracles in the eyes of Pharaoh. He changed his mind and allowed God's people to leave Egypt for their promised land in Canaan (present-day Palestine) to worship their Lord. Pharaoh made promises but then broke those promises several times. Unfortunately, his hardened heart and hard head resulted in his oldest son and his people dying such a terrible death that he reluctantly urged Israel's people to leave his country as soon as possible.

God's miracle finally liberated His people from slavery and a tyrant. However, it was not finished. When all of God's people had fled Egypt and arrived at the Red Sea, they were very embarrassed. They did not know where to go. Should they cross the immense sea, make a right turn, or turn around and go back the way they had come from? They were waiting for the Lord to appear for them in a pillar of cloud or a pillar of fire. They suddenly heard the sounds of galloping and a battle cry. Everyone turned back and saw the cavalry of Egypt's army coming forward toward them.

Had Moses had an experience like this before in his life? No, he had never encountered an event like this. How could he solve such a difficult problem? Would it occur to him to move forward and enter the Red Sea? No. He did not have a ship, boat, canoe, sampan, or any other means of sea transportation. Should they surrender and return to Egypt to become the slaves of Pharaoh as before? No. He could not do that; once they had left, they could not return.

Many people came to rebuke, blame, and accuse Moses of stupidity, dictatorship, and the destruction of the Egyptians. Some said, "Is it because there were no graves in Egypt that you have taken us away to die in the wilderness?... For it would have been better for us to serve the Egyptians than to die in the wilderness" (Exodus 14:11–12).

Knowing the Lord's power and decision, when Moses looked up to see the pillar of cloud still standing in the sky, he calmly said to the people, "The Lord will fight for you while you keep silent" (Exodus 14:14). Read these words from the Lord to understand how the Red Sea became a blessing for the Israelites:

> Why are you crying out to Me? Tell the sons of Israel to go forward. As for you, lift up your staff, and stretch out your hand over the sea and divide it, and the sons of Israel shall go through the midst of the sea on dry land. As for Me, behold, I will harden the hearts of the Egyptians so that they will go in after them; and I will be honored through Pharaoh and all his army, through his chariots and his horsemen. Then the Egyptians will know that I am the Lord, when I am honored through Pharaoh, through his chariots and his horsemen. (Exodus 14:15–18)

The results were the Israelites' success and the Egyptian army's failure. The Israelites survived, and the Egyptian soldiers were dead. The weak lived and the strong died. But what are your thoughts? Who do you think performed the miracle at the Red Sea, the Lord or Moses? Some say the Lord, because He said He would be honored through Pharaoh and his army. But some say Moses obeyed the Lord when he lifted up his staff and stretched out his hand over the sea to divide it. If the Lord performed the miracle, why did He tell Moses to do anything? The Lord told Moses to do those things so that he would be honored through his actions.

Without the Lord's power and His approval, no one can accomplish anything great. The Lord could accomplish the miracle of dividing the sea; however, He wanted to let Moses practice the action or learn how to use his staff so he would know what to do in future situations. Remember: Moses was still a human being; in spite of this experience, he had faults when he came to the wilderness of Zin and stayed at Kadesh. When people complained of the water shortage, the Lord told Moses to take the rod and speak to the rock. Moses could not control his temper; he was so upset that he struck the rock twice instead of just speaking. His deed displeased the Lord, who punished him by not allowing him to enter the Promised Land before his death.

Moses' miracles in front of the Egyptian Pharaoh and the Israelites were accomplished only through the Lord's instruction and order. Moses was just a man—a servant of the Lord; therefore, Moses' miracles were the Lord's miracles for His plan and will.

Miracles Performed through Other Prophets and Apostles

The prophets in the Old Testament had to cope with Israeli leaders, the false prophets, and the people who were not faithful to the Lord but followed the false gods of the Gentiles. All the major prophets and minor prophets were instructed by the Lord to proclaim God's warnings against those who worshiped the Gentile gods and imitated what the Gentiles did. The prophets sometimes performed miracles to help and save the Israelites during their poverty, starvation, and illness.

Prophet Elijah: Prophet Elijah obeyed the Lord and came to the village of Zarephath in order to save a widow's family from famine. He prayed for the widow's son to survive.

Prophet Elisha: This prophet replaced Prophet Elijah, who was taken to heaven without physical death. Elisha performed many miracles:

1. "The water is bad and the land is unfruitful" (2 Kings 2:19). By Elisha's actions and words, the water became

good again: "The waters have been purified to this day" (2 Kings 2:22).

2. Elisha's student passed away. The student's wife was poor, and her lender wanted to take her two children to work as the slaves. She came to the prophet Elisha and spoke of this. The prophet told her to borrow many empty cans and pour oil from a jar into those cans until they were full. (See 2 Kings 4:1–7.) The single jar of oil filled so many cans that when they were sold, the family was able to repay their debt and live on the rest.

3. A Shunammite woman had no children but treated the Prophet Elisha nicely by providing him with a comfortable room to stay in whenever he stopped in that area. He prophesied that she was going to have one son in the next year. The son grew up and became seriously ill and died. The prophet received the news of the woman's son's death, and he prayed until the son rose from the dead. (See 2 Kings 4:8–37.)

4. He transformed poisonous stew into a safe meal. (See 2 Kings 4:38–41.)

5. One man from Baal-shalishah "brought the man of God bread of the first fruits, twenty loads of barley and fresh ears of grain in the sack" (2 Kings 4:42). The prophet commanded, "Give them to the people that they may eat" (2 Kings 4:42). His attendant said, "'What will I set this before a hundred men?'... But he said, 'Give them to the people that they man eat, for thus says the LORD, They shall eat and have some left over'" (2 Kings 4:43–44).

6. General Naaman of Syria was a leper. The prophet Elisha told him to bathe at the Jordan River seven times. He did what the prophet said and was fully healed. (See 2 Kings 5:1–14).

7. Gehazi was the prophet Elisha's servant; he got leprosy from General Naaman because of his greed. (See 2 Kings 5:15–27.)

8. When his students cut down the trees to build houses by the Jordan River, "the axe head fell into the water ... he cut off a stick and threw it in there, and made the iron float" (2 Kings 6:1–7).

9. The king of Aram was told that the prophet Elisha knew of secret tactical plans that Syria had against Israel. "He sent horses and chariots and a great army there, and they came by night and surrounded the city" (2 Kings 6:14.) When the prophet's student was fearful, the prophet said, "Do not fear, for those who are with us are more than those who are with them" (2 Kings 6:16.) Indeed, "the mountain was full of horses and chariots of fire all around Elisha" (2 Kings 6:17.) After the prophet's prayers, the Lord struck the Syrian soldiers with blindness.

The king of Aram was upset and brought all of his nation's army to surround Samaria for a long time to cause a food shortage. The king of Israel came to ask the prophet, "Behold, this evil is from the LORD; why should I wait for the LORD any longer?" (2 Kings 6:33.) The king blamed Elisha's king for the famine that the Israelites experienced. The prophet promised the king of Israel that the famine would stop the following day. Four lepers went from Israel to the Aramaean camps to find food to eat; they found an empty city without an army. "The Lord had caused the army of the Aramaeans to hear a sound of chariots and a sound of horses, even the sound of a great army, so that they said to one another, 'Behold, the king of Israel has hired against us the kings of the Hittites and the kings of the Egyptians, to come upon us.' Therefore they arose and left in the twilight, and left their tents and their horses and their donkeys, even the camp just as it was, and fled for their life" (1 Kings 7:3–7).

The prophet Elisha performed more miracles than the others. He was a very brave prophet, a faithful servant to the Lord, a patriot to Israel, and an honest master with no corruption.

Peter: Peter went with John into the temple in Jerusalem to pray. When they both came to a gate called Beautiful, they met a man who was lame from birth and performed a miracle to help him walk into the temple. (See Acts 3:2–8.)

Another time, Peter came to Lydda and met a man called Aeneas, who was paralyzed. Peter performed a miracle to help him rise and walk. (See Acts 9:32–35.) He also prayed for a woman called Tabitha (in Greek, this is the name "Dorcas"), who died. All the widows wept because they received the tunics and garments from Tabitha when she was still alive and performing "deeds of kindness and charity" for them. After Peter's prayers, Tabitha was resurrected. (See Acts 9:36)

Paul: The Bible records what Paul accomplished: "God was performing extraordinary miracles by the hands of Paul, so that handkerchiefs or aprons were even carried from his body to the sick, and the diseases left them and the evil spirits went out" (Acts 19:11–12).

A Summary

The sentence "God was performing extraordinary miracles by the hands of Paul" (Acts 19:11) describes the miracles through angels and mankind. All miracles are God's work, and God's work is a miracle. Whatever God does is miraculous because it is extraordinary and supernatural. Man cannot perform miracles if God does not work through him. The universe, sun, moon, stars, earth, oceans, mountains, rivers, waterfalls, seas, lakes, animals, and mankind are God's works and miracles. Because of this, I am quite interested in nature. I like to see the various landscapes of nature, such as the beach, waterfalls, rivers, animals, and newborn babies, because they are God's works—God's miracles.

As for me, anything extraordinary and difficult to accomplish is successfully completed thanks to God's help, God's work, and God's miracle. The following stories of my life are true and were difficult to solve, but they were successfully completed without my effort, strength, and skill. I think they were accomplished only through God's miracles. I have written these stories down that you might read and realize that there is a God, our dear Lord, who performs miracles for us to live out the Lord Jesus Christ's statement, "I came that they may have life, and have it abundantly" (John 10:10b.)

Chapter 3
Miracle in God's Will

The will of God caused the works of God. The universe, the earth, and man were created by miracles through God's will. Through God's will, the first marriage in the world was performed in the garden of Eden. God also used Noah to build the ark, according to His will. All the languages of the world were created in God's will during the construction of the Tower of Babel. The call for Abraham to be the ancestor of Israel's people was done in God's will.

God's will is quite different from man's will, or higher than man's will, as the Lord said: "'For My thoughts are not your thoughts, Nor are your ways My ways,' declared the Lord. 'For as the heavens are higher than the earth. So are My ways higher than your ways And My thoughts than your thoughts.'" (Isaiah 55:8–9)

The Creation of the First Couple in the World

The Creation of Adam

The way God created Adam and Eve was quite different from the other acts of creation. God spoke but did not use His hand to do anything when creating the universe, earth, light, and animals. This is the way God created man: "Then the LORD God formed man of dust from the ground, and breathed into his nostrils the breath of life; and man became a living being" (Genesis 2:7.) "God formed man of dust" means He worked by His hand. "He breathed into his nostrils" means He worked by His mouth. Therefore, man's body consists of two parts. The first part—the flesh or body, which returns to the ground after death—belongs to earth: "For you are dust, And to dust you shall return" (Genesis 3:19). The second part—our eternal spiritual substance, or soul— returns to God after death: "Then the dust will return to the earth as it was, and the spirit will return to God who gave it" (Ecclesiastes 12:7.)

You can see God's insight during His creation of man; the use of dust for man's body and His breath for man's living soul were part of a plan against Satan's destruction.

The Creation of Eve

God created man with dust, but He did not follow the same manner in making Eve. He did not use the dust of the ground to make Eve but rather made her in a different way. This way was very interesting and meaningful: "So the Lord God caused a deep sleep to fall upon the man, and he slept; then He took one of his ribs and closed up the flesh at that place. The Lord God fashioned into a woman the rib which He had taken from the man, and brought her to the man. The man said, 'This is now bone of my bones, And flesh of my flesh; She shall be called Woman, Because she was taken out of Man.' For this reason a man shall leave his father and his mother, and be joined to his wife; and they shall become one flesh" (Genesis 2:21–24). God's will was to unite man and woman in a happy marriage. So the husband and the wife must be one, not two persons. The Lord Jesus Christ says, "So they are no longer two, but one flesh. What therefore God has joined together, let no man separate" (Matthew 19:6).

It is very meaningful and interesting to know God's methods for creating a woman using one man's rib and flesh in order that they may be united into one flesh as a married couple. If God created woman as He created man, dust with dust would not join as easily. Praise the Lord for God's miracles in the creation of man and woman. No one can make such a way like God's miracles!

By using such methods for creation, God made the love between a husband and wife so natural that it is hard for them to leave one another, except in the case of separation and divorce. Their love is so sacred and solemn that the Lord wants the couple to live together and depend on each other while combining their possessions and properties.

The Ark of Noah

The Bible says this about the sin of man: "Then the LORD saw that the wickedness of man was great on the earth, and that every intent of the thoughts of his heart was only evil continually. The LORD was sorry that He had made man on the earth, and He was grieved in His heart. The LORD said, 'I will blot out man whom I have created from the face of the land, from man to animals to creeping things and to birds of the sky; for I am sorry that I have made them'" (Genesis 6:5–7).

He was sorry that He had made man and put them on the earth, and He said to Noah, "The end of all flesh has come before Me; for the earth is filled with violence because of them; and behold, I am about to destroy them with the earth" (Genesis 6:13). He said He would destroy man on the earth. He then commanded Noah to build an ark. If He was to destroy man, what was the purpose of His command to Noah to build the ark? He knew Noah was five hundred years old, which made him an old, unhealthy, and slow man. Why did He not use a person better than Noah? Is the answer that "Noah was a righteous man, blameless in his time" (Genesis 6:9) and "Noah found favor in the eyes of the Lord" (Genesis 6:8)? Noah's family was composed of just eight people—four men and four women, including an old couple who often sat in the chairs just to see the others work. Could those elements be the reasons God chose Noah to build the ark?

No. God never depends on human merit to when choosing to use someone in any of His plans. But please read these lines: "By faith Noah, being warned by God about things not yet seen, in reverence prepared an ark for the salvation of his household, by which he condemned the world, and became an heir of the righteousness which is according to faith … and did not spare the ancient world, but preserved Noah, a preacher of righteousness, with seven others, when He brought a flood upon the world of the ungodly" (Hebrews 11:7; 2 Peter 2:5). We can trust in God's choice and should not ask the reason why that choice was made.

Once Noah had two jobs to do, he had a great deal of time to finish the ark. God wanted plenty of time to be given for people to hear Noah's sermons so that they might repent and come into the ark of salvation like Noah's family.

God's heart was grieved because of man's sin. He wanted to teach man a tough lesson along with a test that they must pass: "Do you repent for your sin? If you do, do you want to be saved and come into the ark before the rain pours down on the earth from heaven?" If one repented but did not want to come into the ark, it meant he or she did not trust the Lord and did not really repent. These people's destinies came to an end. If one repented and wanted to come into the ark, he or she was welcome to stay until the flood was over; then he or she would go out of the ark to be called the Lord's children and inherit heaven forever. That was God's will. God used Noah's hands, mind, and family to build the ark, and He used his preaching that man could hear God's warning against those who wanted to be selfish.

Abraham Accepted God's Call

Most Sunday school students, at some point, raise two questions for their teachers to answer and explain regarding Abraham:

1. Why did God choose and call Abraham to be the ancestor of His chosen people?
2. Why did God choose the Israelites to be His chosen people?

The first question is about an individual. The second one is about a group of people. These two questions are connected; once you've answered the first question, you'll have the answer to the second. To answer them, the student needs to read over the Bible to know God's will. And once familiar with God's will, he or she will find it easy to understand God's choice.

First of all, remember that God's choice is never based on human merit. Abraham was not selected because he was worthy; nor were the Israelites called to be God's chosen people because of their worthiness. God can choose anyone and anything He likes. Do not ask why, because "For as the heavens are higher than the earth, So are My ways higher than your ways, And My thoughts than your thoughts" (Isaiah 55:9).

However, Noah and Abraham seemed to have similar values that could be seen as qualifying characteristics for serving God: faith, obedience, and integrity. Noah obeyed the Lord to build the ark immediately, and Abraham obeyed the Lord to promptly leave his country to be the ancestor of the Israelites, and he also offered his son Isaac as a burnt offering at Mount Moriah. The Lord provided a "ram caught in the thicket by his horns" (Genesis 22:13–14) for him to offer to the Lord as a burnt offering.

Noah and Abraham were the Lord's servants, who obeyed and served Him, and God's works were completed in His will:

1. Noah finished the construction, and his whole family of eight people entered the ark, receiving safety and salvation; the flood was made through God's miracle.
2. Abraham obeyed the Lord, bringing his son Isaac to Mount Moriah for an offering. The Lord performed a miracle by showing him a ram in the thicket to use instead.

Joseph and His Dream

The Bible tells the story of Abraham from Genesis chapter twelve to chapter twenty-five and the story of Joseph from chapter thirty-seven to chapter fifty. The Lord mentions the patriarchs of Israel by name—Abraham, Isaac, and Jacob—but Joseph is not listed. However, Joseph was a godly man who was used to perform God's will through God's miracles. In my opinion, Joseph was a typical man in Christ with Christian characteristics and qualifications that God desires.

Joseph was born to Jacob. His father loved him so much that after his mother, Rachel, passed away, he made him a varicolored tunic for him to wear. It was very expensive, of course, for that period of time. This biased father showed favor to Jacob, whom his brothers disliked because of his dreams.

His brothers called him the dreamer when he came to see them. Instead of welcoming Joseph, they threw him into an empty and dry pit. When a caravan of Ishmaelites came from Gilead, the brothers sold Joseph to them, and he was taken to be a slave to Potiphar, an Egyptian officer of Pharaoh and captain of the bodyguard. He gradually became Potiphar's beloved personal servant. The master loved him and used him as a trustworthy servant. During his time there, Potiphar's wife fell in love with the young Hebrew, and her love was strongly rejected by him, as he was a spiritual man of God. She slandered against Joseph so her husband would put him in prison.

Joseph kept silent and did not blame anybody. After some time had passed, he was finally set free to meet with the Egyptian king and interpret his dreams. After observing Joseph's talents, the king used him to manage the nation's economy and administration; his role was much like that of a modern-day prime minister.

Seven years of famine were setting in on the land. Jacob sent his sons to buy grain in Egypt. Joseph recognized his brothers and explained that he was the one they had sold into slavery and that he now served as an official under Pharaoh's command. Joseph wanted his brothers to go back to his homeland and bring his father, his youngest brother, and the whole family to Egypt to live near him.

Joseph's life indicated God's miracles in God's will. Remember the prophecy of Abraham's destiny: "Know for certain that your descendants will be strangers in a land that is not theirs, where they will be enslaved and oppressed four hundred years" (Genesis 15:13). From Abraham to Joseph, four generations passed. the Lord's word had been fulfilled by Joseph's power to bring the whole family to the foreign land and live an abundant life in God's will.

Moses with His Staff

Moses was presented in an earlier chapter as a man who performed miracles by God's approval and power. In this chapter, we'll look at him as a man who was miraculously selected as a child by God to serve Him. The Lord chose and prepared him when he was a newborn to be His servant.

The Bible records the story of how he was picked up by Pharaoh's daughter along the Nile River and nursed by his own mother until he had grown enough to be adopted by Pharaoh's daughter.

He knew he was originally a Hebrew, and he defended a Hebrew and killed an Egyptian. The next day, another Hebrew disclosed that Moses was the one who had killed the Egyptian. Fear arose in Moses, and he ran from the king to Midian, where he married and became a shepherd for his father-in-law, a priest. One day he heard an angel call his name. The angel commanded him not to come any closer but to remove his sandals from his feet, because he was standing on holy ground. The angel and Moses had a conversation about leading the Israelites out of Egypt and into the Promised Land. Moses initially refused to participate in this very difficult mission, but he finally acceded to be the leader of the Israelites and set them free from slavery.

Moses was selected to be God's servant from birth. God prepared him to be accepted at the Nile River by Pharaoh's daughter so that she might take pity on him and adopt him as her son. Moses was brought up in the royal court, received an Egyptian education, and was introduced to their culture so that he would be equipped for his future encounter with Pharaoh.

Moses' life from birth to death was in God's plan, blessed by God's grace, and strengthened by God's miracles by God's will. His was a great man's life established through the plan God had for him and his country. How about the life of a common working man? Does God have such a plan for people like that? We should not humble ourselves so much that we think that God has never paid attention to us. Remember the story of the widow in Zarephath. She was too poor to live two more days after having lunch with her only son, yet God sent the prophet Elijah to help her survive. Our God is love!

David with His Sling

The Lord said to Samuel, "How long will you grieve over Saul, since I have rejected him from being king over Israel? Fill your horn with oil and go; I will send you to Jesse the Bethlehemite, for I have selected a king for Myself among his sons" (1 Samuel 16:1). When he went to Jesse's home and saw Eliab, Samuel thought, "'Surely the Lord's anointed is before Him.' But the Lord said to Samuel, 'Do not look at his appearance or at the height of his stature, because I have rejected him; for God sees not as man sees, for man looks at the outward appearance, but the Lord looks at the heart'" (1 Samuel 16:6–7).

The Lord rejected seven sons of Jesse. "Samuel said to Jesse, 'Are these all the children?' And he said, 'There remains yet the youngest, and behold, he is tending the sheep'" (1 Samuel 16:11). David, Jesse's youngest son, came home from the tending the flock. The Lord said to Samuel, "Arise, anoint him; for this is he" (1 Samuel 16:12). David, rejected by his older family members, was the one the Lord chose to be the second king of Israel. He was brave, nice, loyal to the former king, and a close friend of Jonathan. The Lord performed His miracle through David's hands. He used his skillful talents of the sling to kill Goliath, a Philistine champion, who used to frighten Israel's king, the general, and the soldiers at battle.

In God's will and by God's miracle, David, the rejected candidate of Jesse's family, became the selected king of Israel, who brought more independence, security, glory, and prosperity to the country than it had seen in forty years.

The Apostle Paul

Stephen, a godly Christian, boldly gave an expressive testimony against the Jewish priests, the elders, the scribes, and the council. He was full of the Holy Spirit, gazing "intently into heaven and saw the glory of God, and Jesus standing at the right hand of God; and he said, 'Behold, I see the heavens opened up and the Son of Man standing at the right hand of God.' ... When they had driven him out of the city, they began stoning him; and the witnesses laid aside their robes at the feet of a young man named Saul" (Acts 7:55–58).

This young man named Saul was later known as the apostle Paul. Having been born in a family whose father was a Pharisee (Acts 23:6), Paul was familiar with Greek culture, Roman citizenship, and Hebrew religion. Watching the stoning of Stephen, Paul seemed glad, as he was a leader of a group in active opposition to Christ's religion, called Christianity. He went to Damascus with authority from the high priest to fiercely and violently persecute Christians.

The Lord Jesus Christ met him when he approached Damascus, and he was immediately and miraculously transformed from a persecutor into a man of God. Since then, Paul eagerly and boldly preached, stating, "Yet we do speak wisdom among those who are mature; a wisdom, however, not of this age nor of the rulers of this age, who are passing away; but we speak God's wisdom in a mystery, the hidden wisdom which God predestined before the ages to our glory; the wisdom which none of the rulers of this age understood; for if they had understood it they would not have crucified the Lord of glory" (1 Corinthians 2:6–8).

It is not hard to understand why God chose Noah, Abraham, Joseph, and David to be His servants; but it is not easy to understand why the Lord selected this strong persecutor to serve Him during the start of evangelism in the world.

This was God's miracle; it was not brought about by human wisdom, strength, position, money, or plan. God's miracles can do anything with anyone and at any time. Man's power cannot do so.

A Summary

God's miracles were performed through the selection of His servants that He used for His will. God's method of choosing those who would serve him is different from our human methods. He selected servants without consideration of their outside appearance. He chose aging men, a newborn baby, a rejected candidate, and even an enemy against Him. Noah was called to build the ark when he was five hundred years old. Abraham was called to leave his country when he was seventy-five years old. The newborn baby Moses was picked up by Pharaoh's daughter and nursed by his own mother. The rejected candidates, Joseph and David, were rejected by their family members and later became very important people in Egypt and Israel. Paul was a former persecutor against Christianity and later became an excellent missionary and epistle writer.

Man could not accomplish such things, because they are too hard. Only God could accomplish the things mentioned earlier. God's miracles are perfect and wonderful, allowing us to praise the Lord for His power and His will.

Chapter 4
Miracle for God's Compassion

The key verse in the entire Bible is "For God so loved the world, that He gave His only begotten Son, that whoever believes in Him shall not perish, but have eternal life" (John 3:16).

The Lord Jesus Christ's disciples followed Him for some years, realizing that "seeing the people, He felt compassion for them, because they were distressed and dispirited like sheep without a shepherd" (Matthew 9:36).

Stories in both the Old Testament and the New Testament indicate God's love and mercy. God loves everyone, not only His own people; he showed love to the Gentiles. He does not like to see oppression, unfairness, or unjust actions taken among His children or the Gentiles. He loves the poor, orphans, widows, prisoners, money borrowers, patients, the homeless, strangers, and sufferers.

God commands His children to also love those whom He loves. These verses tell us what God wants us to do: "Now when you reap the harvest of your land, you shall not reap to the very corners of your field, nor shall you gather the gleanings of your harvest. Nor shall you glean your vineyard, nor shall you gather the fallen fruit of your vineyard; you shall leave them for the needy and for the stranger. I am the Lord your God" (Leviticus 19:9–10). The Lord teaches how to behave toward foreigners: "When a stranger resides with you in your land, you shall not do him wrong. The stranger who resides with you shall be to you as the native among you, and you shall love him as yourself, for you were aliens in the land of Egypt; I am the Lord your God" (Leviticus 19:33–34).

The following stories will prove what the Lord taught.

Hagar and Ismael

In Genesis 21:9–13, after Isaac was born, Sarah told Abraham to drive out Hagar and her son Ismael. God knew Abraham's heart was broken because he loved both Hagar and Ismael. God comforted him: "Do not be distressed because of the lad and your maid; whatever Sarah tells you, listen to her, for through Isaac your descendants shall be named. And of the son of the maid I will make a nation also, because he is your descendant" (Genesis 21:12–13).

God never urged Abraham to marry Hagar, but Sarah did. She now hated Hagar and her son because Sarah saw Hagar's son, "whom she had borne to Abraham, mocking" (Genesis 21:9). The Lord is a faithful God; "having loved His own who were in the world, He loved them to the end" (John 13:1b), and "Jesus Christ is the same yesterday and today and forever" (Hebrews 13:8).

Leah

In Genesis 29:26–35, we are told that Jacob loved Rachel and worked seven years without salary for Laban, his uncle.

During the first night of marriage with Rachel, Jacob slept with Leah instead of Rachel, through a plan Laban had laid out. The next morning, Jacob angrily asked his uncle, now his father-in-law, why he had been deceived in this way. Laban answered that the local country's law never allowed the younger sister to be married before her older sister. (See Genesis 29:26.) Both Jacob and Rachel mistreated Leah, who had only been acting according to her father's plan.

The Lord saw this unfair behavior and favored her by giving her four sons in four pregnancies: "Now the Lord saw that Leah was unloved, and He opened her womb, but Rachel was barren" (Genesis 29:31). To give thanks to the Lord for His love and favor, she named each of her sons as such:

1. Reuben, the first son: "Because the Lord has seen my affliction; surely now my husband will love me" (Genesis 29:32).
2. Simeon, the second son: "Because the Lord has heard that I am unloved, He has therefore given me this son also" (Genesis 29:33).
3. Levi, the third son: "Now this time my husband will become attached to me, because I have borne him three sons" (Genesis 29:34).
4. Judah, the fourth son: "This time I will praise the LORD" (Genesis 29:35).

The Israelites

In Exodus 1–3, Moses escaped from Egypt to the land of Midian, met the daughters of Jethro, and helped them to get water. He then married Zipporah, Jethro's daughter, and had one son named Gershom. He worked for his father-in-law, a priest of Midian, as a shepherd.

The kings, who formerly knew Joseph very well, had all passed away. The new kings had forgotten what Joseph did for their country and put such bondage upon the Israelites that they cried out. Their cry rose up to God: "So God heard their groaning; and God remembered His covenant with Abraham, Isaac, and Jacob. God saw the sons of Israel, and God took notice of them" (Exodus 2:24–25).

The Lord said to Moses while he was pasturing the flock in front of the blazing fire,

> I have surely seen the affliction of My people who are in Egypt, and have given heed to their cry because of their taskmasters, for I am aware of their sufferings. So I have come down to deliver them from the power of the Egyptians, and to bring them up from that land to a good and precious land, to a land flowing with milk and honey, to the place of the Canaanite and the Hittite and the Amorite and the Perizzite and the Hivite and the Jebusite. Now, behold, the cry of the sons of Israel has come to Me; furthermore, I have seen the oppression with which the Egyptians are oppressing them. (Exodus 3:7–9)

God's miracles encouraged Moses to play the role of Israel's leader, talk to Pharaoh, lead his people out of bondage, travel through the wilderness, and reach the border of the Promised Land.

God's miracles had helped the Israelites for forty years in the wilderness, as recorded:

> Then it shall come about when the LORD your God brings you into the land which He swore to your fathers, Abraham, Isaac and Jacob, to give you, great and splendid cities which you did not build, and

houses full of all good things which you did not fill, and hewn cisterns which you did not dig, vineyards and olive trees which you did not plant, and you eat and are satisfied, then watch yourself, that you do not forget the LORD who brought you from the land of Egypt, out of the house of slavery. You shall fear only the LORD your God; and you shall worship Him and swear by His name. You shall not follow other gods, any of the gods of the peoples who surround you, for the Lord your God in the midst of you is a jealous God; otherwise the anger of the LORD your God will be kindled against you, and He will wipe you off the face of the earth. (Deuteronomy 6:10–15)

Naomi

Unfortunately, Naomi's husband and two sons died. The three women of the family became widows. But one day Naomi heard the good news of the famine ending in her homeland. She decided to return home from Moab. She said good-bye to her daughters-in-law and told them to stay and remarry. They wept bitterly. One woman, Orpha, kissed her and left her. Only Ruth stayed with her, and she said, "Do not urge me to leave you or turn back from following you; for where you go, I will go, and where you lodge, I will lodge. Your people shall be my people, and your God, my God. Where you die, I will die, and there I will be buried. Thus may the LORD do to me, and worse, if anything but death parts you and me" (Ruth 1:16–17).

The mother-in-law of Israel with the daughter-in-law of Moab returned to Bethlehem, Judah for resettlement. Ruth "went and gleaned in the field after the reapers; and she happened to come to the portion of the field belonging to Boaz, who was of the family of Elimelech" (Ruth 2:3). Boaz later married Ruth. They were rich. Ruth was pregnant and gave birth to Obed, the father of Jesse. And Jesse was the father of David.

The book of Ruth records the origin of King David's immediate ancestors. His great-grandfather was Ruth's husband, Boaz. The story reads like a legend that shows the very beautiful behavior of a Moabite woman. Her husband's death and her mother-in-law's agreement allowed her legally marry for a second time. But she insisted on accompanying Naomi to a foreign land, where she might encounter many difficulties and differences, such as language, culture, occupation, food, and religion. Why did she want to take on the heavy burden of nursing an old woman who was not her own mother, in a land where she had no relatives or old friends?

God's miracle was his compassion for Naomi, who had suffered a great deal in the deaths of three dear men—a husband and two sons—in a strange land. God gave Ruth to Naomi as a gift of comfort. When Ruth gave birth to a son named Obed, "The neighbor women gave him a name, saying, 'A son has been born to Naomi!'" (Ruth 4:17). Obed, King David's grandfather, was a reward for both Naomi and Ruth. God's miracles were performed as a compassion for the poor and sufferers, who were faithful to Him, receiving the blessings from heaven.

The Widow in Zarephath

In 1 Kings 17:8–16, an unknown widow and her baby son were living in poverty in the village of Zarephthath. They had enough food for just one meal, and then they would die. The Prophet Elijah told the widow to bake for him one piece of bread, but she replied that she would have only enough food for her family each day. But she did what the prophet told her to do. And indeed she still had enough food for her family every day during the long drought.

God's performed a miracle for the widow's family so they would have food through the drought, because He loved them. Without that miracle, they would not have survived, as they were too poor. The Lord is a God of compassion for all the sufferers in the world. Why don't you ask Him to help you during any poverty or health problems you may experience? I believe God will surely hear your prayers and answer you immediately.

The Widow in Nain

In Luke 7:11–17, the Lord Jesus Christ arrived with His disciples in the city of Nain and suddenly saw the funeral of a young man. The young man's mother was a widow, and he was her only son. You know her special situation: no husband, and now no son. Her only son's death meant that she was broke with no hope, joy, or peace—nothing for her to rely on for a better life. We do not know if she already had a plan of suicide in her mind following her son's death. Many women have such thoughts and actually commit suicide.

God knows everything, including the events surrounding the funeral in Nain. The Lord Jesus Christ, the Prince of Peace, came to help. He told some people who were helping with the burial to stop so that He could do something for him. Then he called him to rise. The young man rose, and the Lord delivered that boy to his mother.

He sees every man in the world. In spite of the fact that there are seven billion people on the earth, God can supernaturally see each individual and help solve any problem, even the transformation between death and life. You see, when anyone has died and then survives, God wants that individual to see his (or her) mother. God's miracle for the lad's resurrection was purposely and intentionally for the mother. When the Lord Jesus first saw the funeral and the mother's tears, "He felt compassion for her, and said to her, 'Do not weep'" (Luke 7:13). The Bible continues with verses 15–16: "The dead man sat up and began to speak. And Jesus gave him back to his mother. Fear gripped them all, and they began glorifying God, saying, 'A great prophet has risen among us!' and, 'God has visited His people!'"

We do not know how long he had been dead, but "The dead man sat up" means he was resurrected from the dead. This event happened so that the crowd could see God's miracle performed by the Lord Himself because "He felt compassion for her" (Luke 7:13).

The Man Blind from Birth

In John 9, the Lord Jesus Christ and His disciples were walking on the road and saw a man blind from birth. They asked Him, "Rabbi, who sinned, this man or his parents, that he would born blind?" The Lord immediately answered them, "It has neither that this man sinned, nor his parents; but it was so that the works of God might be displayed in him" (John 9:1–3). Then "He spat on the ground, and made clay of the spittle, and applied the clay to his eyes, and said to him 'Go, wash in the pool of Siloam.' So he went away and washed, and came back seeing" (John 9:6–7).

This story is similar to that of the widow in Nain. Neither the widow nor the man ever asked the Lord Jesus Christ for help. And no one came to talk to Him about the widow's situation or the blind man's suffering. However, the Lord Himself saw them and had compassion for them. His compassion made him do good deeds without any requests or calling, simply out of "love" (John 3:16, 1 John 4:8–9).

These are the lessons to learn from this passage:

1. The ordinary thought surrounding a bad event was that it was the consequence of a past bad deed and that someone

caused the bad event to happen. This can be phrased as "Reap what you sow." The Bible states, "Do not be deceived, God is not mocked; for whatever a man sows, this he will also reap. For the one who sows to his own flesh will from the flesh reap corruption, but the one who sows to the Spirit will from the Spirit reap eternal life" (Galatians 6:7–8).

2. "Reap what you sow" was also a basic Buddhist doctrine. The founder of Buddhism, Prince Siddharta Gautama, of the Shakya tribe in northern India (now Nepal) was born around 500 BC. At the age of twenty-nine, he witnessed several events that made him think a great deal about life, and he pondered things such as sickness, old age, death, past life, and the next life.

His father, who did not like to see him spend time just thinking of such things but thought he should focus on the future rule of the country as a king on the throne, wanted him to marry. He obeyed his father and later became a father of one child. Yet he was still interested in the unanswered questions: Where did man come from? What is man born for? Why does man become old? Why does man die? Where do the dead go after death?

Those questions urged him to leave the palace at nighttime to find a monk teacher who could give him the answers. But he was unsatisfied, because no one could answer the "why" questions. Then one day he sat down at a banyan tree for meditation, thinking of his personal destiny in the past, in the present, and in the future. Another idea came to him when he thought of sowing and reaping. Once a seed of corn is sown, the corn naturally grows, and it will produce corn, not other fruit.

Buddhism says that Siddharta Gautama was enlightened at that tree and became the founder of Buddhism, with the basic doctrine centered on sowing and reaping, or causes and results. Buddhist doctrine explains that the current life of someone is the result of the previous life, and that the next life will be the result of the current life.

When the Lord Jesus Christ's disciples asked Him a question concerning the past life and the current life, they wanted to bring up the matter of cause and consequence, or sowing and reaping. In this case, they wanted to know who had caused a man to be blind from birth. Did he sin, or did a relative of his—such as his father, mother, or someone else—sin in the past?

This problem related to Buddhism. The disciples were very interested to hear the Lord's answer: "It was neither that this man sinned, nor his parents" (John 9:3a). This answer so far indicates that being blind from birth is not the consequence of a sin in a past life or a sin of any man or person. This man did not sin in his past life; nor did his parents. Neither the blind man nor his parents had past lives; the Bible never mentions reincarnation.

The Lord continued to explain: "it was so that the works of God might be displayed in him" (John 9:3b). The reason he was blind from birth was not because of his sin but because of God's works in him. What were God's works in him? The Lord Jesus Christ immediately spat on the ground, made clay of the spittle, and applied the clay to the blind man's eyes; He then told him to wash his eyes in the pool of Siloam. The man obeyed, and afterward he could see. His blindness had been healed.

After the man's eyes were completely healed, his neighbors and the Pharisees were so surprised that they asked him many times about the one who had healed his eyes. It was a miracle. Christ had performed that miracle for the blind man, but the man's neighbors and the Pharisees accused the Lord of being a sinner, a bad man, because he had performed this miracle on the Sabbath.

Listen to what the blind man said to those who opposed the Lord: "Well, here is an amazing thing, that you do not know where He is from, and yet He opened my eyes. We know that God does not hear sinners; but if anyone is God-fearing and does His will, He hears him. Since the beginning of time it has never been heard that anyone opened the eyes of a person born blind. If this man were not from God, He could do nothing" (John 9:30–33).

The Lord's disciples understood the reason why the man was blind from birth and why "the works of God might be displayed in him" (John 9:3). The man was blind to teach them the following:

1. God performed this miracle for compassion. The Lord saw the man's affliction and performed a miracle to heal him.
2. God performed this miracle for the man so the man could give a wonderful testimony about God's works for him.
3. God performed this miracle for the atheists and the Pharisees, so they might see God's power through the Lord they rejected.
4. God performed this miracle so the man could accept the Lord Jesus Christ as his own Savior: "'Lord, I believe.' And he worshipped Him" (John 9:38).

A Summary

God performs miracles because the Lord feels compassion for those who suffer from poverty, disease, oppression, discrimination, imprisonment, isolation, separation, and many other situations that go unheeded by anyone in the world. People who received healing, gifts, help, or saving from God's miracles usually became God's children through their acceptance of the Lord Jesus Christ as their personal Savior.

Chapter 5
Miracle for God's Penalty

We discussed that God performs miracles out of compassion for those suffering, but God also performs His miracles to punish the wicked, who do evil things in spite of God's warnings. As you read the Bible, you will see numerous occasions on which something bad occurs to a sinner who ignored what the Lord said, despite a promise of penalty for disobeying.

Adam and Eve

In Genesis 3, Adam and Eve looked at the fruit in the middle of the garden with a will of self-satisfaction, not with a heart of obedience. They took, tasted, and ate it, although they knew the consequence of disobedience against God; they knew there would be a consequence. The consequence was dire: pain during childbirth, working hard for a living, and death at the end of earthly life. The people that followed after them also tasted suffering, as they followed in their ancestors' footsteps rather than following God's commands. The Bible says, "All of us like sheep have gone astray, Each of us has turned to his own way; But the LORD has caused the iniquity of us all to fall on Him" (Isaiah 53:6).

Cain

In Genesis 4, the first son of Adam followed his father through his disobedience against the Lord's warning: You must master your countenance; otherwise, "sin is crouching at the door" (Genesis 4–7). Indeed Cain sinned through murder, and the penalty described was so tough that he lamented, "'My punishment is too great to bear!'" (Genesis 4:13).

The People in Noah's Time

In Genesis 6–8, the Bible says the Lord felt sorry that He created human beings on the earth, because "the wickedness of man was great on the earth, and that every intent of the thoughts of his heart was only evil continually" (Genesis 6:5). The Lord reduced the age of the oldest person to 120, instead of nearly 1,000—Adam's age in Genesis chapter 5.

What sin did the people of Noah's time commit? "The sons of God saw that the daughters of man were beautiful; and they took wives for themselves, whomever they chose" (Genesis 6:2). Who were the sons of God? And who were the daughters of man? Were they human or spiritual? Why was God upset when they were married?

This is a tough question for even Biblical scholars to answer. There are various interpretations for this Scripture, but it is up to you to determine which interpretation you agree with.

1. The first interpretation: The sons of God were the angels, who were sent to serve the Lord among human beings. And they loved and married each other. The daughters of man were the children of human beings. They were different in many aspects: physical body, language, work,

way of life, and culture. They could not live as one family. This made God sorry because it was very complicated.

2. The second interpretation: The sons of God were heroes who were strong and skillful at war, such as Samson and the Nephilim. They were created for God to use as bodyguards for the very important people God used as His servants. But during Noah's time, these men married and did not serve God.

3. The third interpretation: The sons of God were the sons of Seth, the third son of Adam and Eve. (See Genesis 4:25.) These people were chosen to be the holy people of God. The daughters of man were the children of Cain. The people born from Seth and Cain married each other. This made God very sorry.

For me, the first interpretation is not practical, because the angels were genderless, incapable of reproducing with mankin. Therefore that interpretation is not reasonable.

The second interpretation implies that the angels were used only for fighting. That is not reasonable, because God is powerful and almighty. He did not need a bodyguard or security. No one can step into heaven without permission from Him. Remember the parable of the wedding banquet for the prince. The king asked one man, "Friend, how did you come in here without wedding clothes?" (Matthew 22:12). God does not need anyone to fight for Him.

The third interpretation is reasonable: The sons of Seth married the daughters of Cain; the holy people married the sinful people. Later in Scripture, the Lord shows that he does not want the Israelite children to marry the Gentiles, so the people of God can remain holy.

Why did God consider marriage so important that He was grieved in His heart and declared, "I will blot out man whom I have created from the face of the land, from man to animals to creeping things and to birds of the sky; for I am sorry that I have made them" (Genesis 6:7)?

The Nazirites' strict instruction for Judge Samson was "No razor shall come upon his head, for the boy shall be a Nazirite to God from the womb; and he shall begin to deliver Israel from the hands of the Philistines" (Judges 13:5). But Samson disclosed the secret of his supernatural strength, and he was seized, imprisoned, and his eyes were gouged out. It became a game for the Philistines to laugh at a champion of Israel.

King Ahab's wife, Jezebel, who threatened to kill the prophet Elijah in twenty-four hours, made a plan to kill Naboth of Jezreel and purposely occupy his vineyard. Herodias, Philip's wife, who committed adultery with King Herod, caused the death of John the Baptist through the nice dance of her daughter. King Solomon, who was influenced by his Gentile wives, made the altars for people's worship and committed the sin of idolatry against God.

The marriage between the sons of God and the daughters of man displeased God so much that He would "blot out man whom He has created from the face of the land" (Genesis 6:7). The big flood of water that came upon the earth destroyed everything, from people to animals, except Noah's family.

People of the Tower of Babel

In Genesis 11:1–9, after the flood, people moved east and settled at a plain in the land of Shinar. They learned to use brick and tar for house construction. This new invention encouraged them to build a city and a very high tower. This allowed them to stay together and prevented them from being "scattered abroad over the face of the whole earth" (Genesis 11:4). The purpose of the city and the tower was to allow them to stay together and make for themselves a name. (See Genesis 11:4.)

The people's project displeased God for three reasons: (1) God wanted them to scatter, which they ignored, staying at a fixed place and not moving anywhere; (2) they made for themselves a name and were proud of themselves, which God disliked, as God wanted them to be humble; and (3) God had promised no more flooding of the earth in the future, but they built a very high tower for their protection, as they did not trust in God's word. Therefore God was angry and performed a miracle, which used different languages to destroy theirs, causing their misunderstanding of each other. As a penalty for their ignorance of God's instruction and warning, the project was not completed.

Sodom and Gomorrah

In Genesis 18:1–29, Lot, Abraham's nephew, moved to settle in the area of Sodom after leaving Abraham's family. He married and became the father of two very wealthy daughters in the city of Sodom. God said to Abraham, "The outcry of Sodom and Gomorrah is indeed great, and their sin is exceedingly grave" (Genesis 18:20).

Thinking of Lot's destiny, Abraham asked God to forgive his nephew and cancel the plan of destruction for Sodom and Gomorrah: "Will You indeed sweep away the righteous with the wicked?" (Genesis 18:23a). He argued with God about the number of righteous people in Sodom and begged for the forgiveness of Sodom's people, including his nephew. But God decided to burn Sodom, in spite of the presence of Lot's family in the sinning city.

However, God remembered Abraham and saved Lot's family members, who obeyed the Lord's command during the escape from the city. The Bible's description of the destruction of the cities is very serious: "The sun had risen over the earth when Lot came to Zoar. Then the Lord rained on Sodom and Gomorrah brimstone and fire from the LORD out of heaven, and He overthrew those cities, and all the valley, and all the inhabitants of the cities, and what grew on the ground. But his wife, from behind him, looked back, and she became a pillar of salt" (Genesis 19:23–26).

The brimstone rain on Sodom and Gomorrah was God's miracle in response to His anger against the wicked and evil city.

The Egyptian Army's Death at the Red Sea

In Exodus 14:1–31, after the death of the oldest son of the Egyptians in Egypt, Pharaoh agreed with Moses to set the Israelites free to return to their homeland in Palestine. However, when Israel's people went out of Egypt, Pharaoh and his servants changed their attitude toward the Israelites and said, "What is this we have done, that we have let Israel go from serving us?" (Exodus 14:5). So Pharaoh commanded his whole army to "chase after them with all the horses and chariots of Pharaoh, his horsemen and his army, and they overtook them camping by the sea, beside Pi-hahiroth, in front of Baal-zephon" (Exodus 14:9).

The Lord had killed all the oldest sons of the Egyptians to prove His power to the rebellious people. But they did not realize that Israel's people had left Egypt for freedom. If they continued to take them back into slavery, their God might be angry and could damage their country. They depended on their powerful army, which had horses and chariots, and thought that Israel had no defenses against the soldiers' attacks. They thought they might kill the Israelites for the revenge of their oldest sons' deaths.

If someone with a neutral attitude was standing at the Red Sea and watched this scene unfold—the Israelites walking safely and peacefully through the walls of water, the Egyptian army running toward the Red Sea—he would be so fearful for Israel's people. Thousands of soldiers were chasing aging people, women, children, the sick, and the pregnant. It must have looked like a dire situation for Israel. One strong champion was going to defeat one weak baby!

Remember: the Lord was commanding the battle! After the last group from Israel went out of the Red Sea, the Lord said to Moses, "Stretch out your hand over the sea so that the waters may come back over the Egyptians, over their chariots and their horsemen" (Exodus 14:26). The Lord killed all of the Egyptian soldiers in the midst of the sea. If someone with a neutral attitude was present to watch this scene, he would be afraid no longer for Israel but for the Egyptian army, which was destroyed by a powerful God who protected the weak to defeat the strong.

It was God's miracle through this penalty. Israel's people sang the victory song with the staff of Moses: "The Lord is a warrior; The Lord is His name. Pharaoh's chariots and his army He has cast into the sea, and the choicest of his officers are drowned in the Red Sea. The deeps cover them; They went down into the depths like a stone" (Exodus 15:3–5).

The Prophet Jonah in the Stomach of a Great Fish

In Jonah 1:1–17, the Lord told the prophet Jonah to complete an overseas mission in a great city called Nineveh. His mission was to preach to the wicked people because they sinned against the Lord. Jonah seemed to have little love for that city, and he did not do what the Lord told him.

He went to Joppa, where there was a harbor. He paid for a ticket to take a ship to Tarshish instead of Nineveh. The two cities were far from each other. We do not know what he was going to do in Tarshish or why he did not obey the Lord.

The Bible describes Jonah's action like this: "Jonah had gone below into the hold of the ship, lain down and fallen sound asleep. So the captain approached him and said, 'How is it that you are sleeping? Get up, call on your god. Perhaps your god will be concerned about us so that we will not perish'" (Jonah 1:5–6).

Jonah woke up and heard that a great storm was striking the ship. The sailors asked everyone to pray to his god, if each man's god could help. In addition, they threw the cargo out of the ship to lighten it. Unfortunately there was no way to save the ship from sinking. They finally cast lots to "'learn on whose account this calamity has struck us' So they cast lots and the lot fell on Jonah" (Jonah 1:7).

Jonah intentionally made a flight from the Lord's presence, hoping to escape from the mission in Nineveh. But "Where can I go from Your Spirit? Or where can I flee from Your presence? If I ascend to heaven, You are there; If I make my bed in Sheol, behold, You are there. If I take the wings of the dawn, If I dwell in the remotest part of the sea, Even there Your hand will lead me, And Your right hand will lay hold of me" (Psalm 139:7–10).

Jonah knew the Lord had found him on the ship headed to another city—not Nineveh, as He had commanded. Jonah was thrown into the ocean. The Lord prepared a great fish to swallow him and keep him in its stomach for three days and three nights. That was God's miracle through penalty for a prophet who disobeyed Him.

The Lord loved, but never favored, His servant who disobeyed Him. The Bible also presents some of His servants who displeased Him and received serious punishments. Samson, a Nazarite, fell in love with a Gentile woman and was punished by imprisonment, the loss of his eyes, and death. Achan stole trophies of war at Jericho and was executed. The children in a state of chaos seriously punished King David, who killed Uriah the Hittite to take his wife, Bathsheba. Judas Iscariot betrayed the Lord Jesus Christ and committed suicide.

A Summary

God purposely performed miracles for penalty to those who displeased and disobeyed Him. Many people received punishments from the Lord because they betrayed, ignored, or despised Him. The apostle Paul teaches, "Do not be deceived, God is not mocked; for whatever a man sows, this he will also reap" (Galatians 6:7). Be careful, try your best to show your loyalty to the Lord, and try to please Him with your best service and obedience.

Section II

God's Miracles for My Civilian Life

Chapter 6

The First Miracle: No More Poverty

The Poverty of an Unhealthy Boy

My parents gave birth to thirteen children, and I was the seventh one. Five of them died during childhood because of my family's poverty and the short supply of medications during the Second World War. As for me, my mother later said to me that I probably would not live past three years old. My body was so skinny it looked like a skeleton. When I walked, some people sadly said, "Look! A skeleton is walking!"

My parents were uneducated and married in their teenage years; Father was almost twenty years old; Mother, nineteen. My father's salary from the French Army was very low; it could not provide for our big family. The lack of funds largely contributed to my unhealthy state, because of the poor nutrition I received.

My family's poverty caused my father to leave his hometown for Soc Trang, a larger city, where he could start a small business. My older sister, fourteen years old; my older brother, eight years old; and I, six years old, stayed in the village because our father's wooden boat was too small to carry all the family members for a long-distance trip on the river.

My brother and I often went to school without breakfast. I was unable to walk home after school; my brother and one of my classmates carried me home almost every day. Schoolchildren during French rule had two days off a week—Thursday and Sunday. My sister woke us up to walk from home to the beach so that we could find clams and shellfish that we might sell. My sister dug the ground with her shovel, and my brother and I separated the soil to find the shells.

On some days, we didn't have any food for meals. I once went down the riverbank, where carriers were preparing to take small crabs off the boats to transport them to stores for sale. I boldly asked the carriers, "Gentlemen, please give us some crabs and water for my brother and me to have food for lunch today."

Looking at me with a little surprise, one of the carriers asked, "Where are your parents, and why don't you have food for lunch?"

I answered, "My parents are now in the big city doing some small business, and they did not have money to give us for living." They looked at one another, and they finally gave me some small crabs, fearing their supervisors would check.

My parents were given some news about us from their former neighbors in town. Because I looked so weak, they said that I would die soon if I were not taken to live beside them for care. In 1946, my sister prepared for us to leave my parents' hometown of Vinh Chau for Soc Trang, where I continued to live until 1980, when I crossed the Pacific Ocean to resettle in the United States of America.

My sister, my brother, and I shared a wooden boat on a long journey to meet my parents, sisters, and brother. The boat was powered not by an engine but by a sail and oars. They were so touched and thrilled when they saw us. My mother looked so sad; I saw her tears rolling down her cheeks. However, we all were joyful to be reunited, albeit still in poverty. We, the children, did not go to school, because of the guerrilla warfare between Viet Minh and the French Army; all the schools were closed for a while.

My parents' boat was too small for the whole family to sleep in overnight. The boys had to find a covered place at the market to sleep. The police officers once found us during their patrol around the city and ordered us to leave the market right away. We immediately took our blankets and pillows and left with our anxiety and embarrassment. That night we wandered, remaining awake until the sunrise.

The next day, we traveled a long distance from the heart of the city to a farm outside the city, where we asked the farmers to give us a place on their house porch for us to sleep overnight. They agreed, provided we would water all the vegetables on their farm. We agreed with them. In the event of rain, we would stay on the house porch for many hours.

My father had nothing to do to earn a living, so he pulled a two-wheeled cart that contained bananas, sugar cane, coconuts, and oranges from the stores to the bus station for the customers. I stayed where he could find me, so he could hand me a bag of rice after he got some money from his customer. I would bring it home for my mother to cook for the whole family. One day, a sad thing happened. He gave me a bag of rice, and I held it, but my long, sharp nails tore the paper bag, and some rice dropped out and fell on the ground. He slapped my face with such heaviness that I cried and ran away from him. I stayed at my friend's house all day.

Poverty caused sadness, but sadness mysteriously switched to happiness when a good education and God's involvement showed in the personal life of His children. It was like the Israelites' cry under the bondage of the Egyptians. He heard the cry and immediately solved the problem by talking to Moses to free them.

Then He began performing His miracles for Moses to do what He commanded. And that was my experience!

One day I babysat for my mother so she could do her business at the fruit market. When I held my youngest brother of ten months old, I suddenly saw my father pulling his two-wheel cart full of fruit. I could feel that he was exhausted while pulling the cart on the slope. I slapped a tree, saying to myself, "Minh, try to study hard to earn money, in order that your parents do not have to work hard like this in the future."

Poverty encouraged me to make efforts in my education and toiling. Indeed I tried my best at school and even at home to fight my poverty. One of my teachers was aware of my efforts and said to me, "Minh, your health is not good. Do not try to study so hard that you might get sick. You should think of your health."

I passed the examination for my elementary school graduation in 1952. After four years, I passed another examination for my middle school graduation in 1957. My older brother came from Saigon to take me with him so that I might continue my education.

My parents' family. I am the second from left, with glasses, in the fifth row.

I passed the tests that allow selected students to attend two vocational schools in Saigon: the National Commerce School and the National Pedagogy School. The National Commerce School required three years of attendance, and the National Pedagogy School required only one year. I went to the National Commerce School for one month and left it for the National Pedagogy School, where I continued to study until graduation.

I was unhealthy and poor, but the Lord knew my circumstance, heard my prayers, and allowed me to pass the tests required for the two vocational schools. It was then my choice to pursue the school that best fit my interests. I preferred teaching, so it was a clear choice as to which school I should stay with The Lord really did me a favor by giving me some professional occupations. Both were good in salary and job security. Praise the Lord for His love, help, and blessing!

I knew that my knowledge and talent were not good enough to pass the tough tests or to merit a good teaching position in the public sector. However, I had a few secrets to win the competition, and those were prayers and basing my decisions on key verses I had memorized since my boyhood:

> Then he said to me, "This is the word of the Lord to Zerubbabel saying, Not by might nor by power, but by My Spirit", says the Lord of hosts. (Zechariah 4:6)

> Is anything too difficult for the LORD? (Genesis 18:14a)

> But He said, "The things that are impossible with people are possible with God." (Luke 18:27)

If Noah and his family members could make the ark, Israelites could cross the Red Sea, Jericho could fall down without manpower, Goliath could be killed by David, all the prison gates could be opened for Peter to go home, a great earthquake could come to set free the prisoners and save the whole family of the jailor in the prison of Philippi, a paralytic could pick up a pallet and walk, and a blind man could see, then a poor and unhealthy student like me could be selected to attend both the government vocational schools.

One interesting thing happened that encouraged me during my depression and anxiety. Several days before the exam for the National Commerce School, I knelt down and prayed, "Oh Lord, please help me in this upcoming competition. Thousands of candidates will take the exam, but only sixty students will be selected. How could I be selected? It is very tough and hard to be selected. Without your help, I will be ashamed."

The exam consisted of three subjects in two kinds of test: a written test consisting of a Vietnamese essay, a foreign language test in either French or English, and a mathematics test, as well as an oral test on mathematics.

After the exam, I saw my name on the list for the oral test. I did not know how many candidates took the oral test. When my name was called, I entered the room with confidence. The examiner asked one question, which I immediately solved on the blackboard using trigonometry; it was not in the curriculum for this exam level. This surprised the teacher, and he said, "I will tell the board to select you!"

Several days later, I came to the National Commerce School for the result of the exam. I saw my name on the list of the selected students, and I was ranked number forty-six out of sixty. The school selected sixty candidates. Number forty-six was the exact number I saw in my dream some days before the exam! The Lord had let me see in a dream, before I took the exam, that I would be selected by the National Commerce School.

I can imagine how much sorrow I would have if I had failed all the exams for vocational school. My parents, brothers, and sisters would have felt disappointed to see all hope disappear from our poor family. God wanted us, His new believers, to rely on Him in every circumstance in order to learn that God is omnipotent, omnipresent, and omniscient, as recorded: "I will give thanks to You, for I am fearfully and wonderfully made; Wonderful are Your works, And my soul knows it very well" (Psalm 139:14). Since He has those characteristics, we should not worry but should truly trust in Him forever.

Chapter 7
Some Extraordinary Happenings

We Got Saved!

Three people living in my parents' home worked so hard day and night, yet they could not afford the family's needs. My father wanted to switch to running a small business instead of pulling the fruit cart for customers. But how could he when he did not have enough capital to start a small business? He thought of borrowing money from someone. One day, he went to one of his hometown friend Mr. Sau. Following is the conversation between Mr. Sau and my father at Mr. Sau's home.

My father said, "Hi, Mr. Sau. How are you?"

"Fine. And you? What can I do for you, Mr. Cam?"

"I want to ask you to lend me some money for a small business."

"How much?" said Mr. Sau."

"Five thousand piasters" my father said.

"Okay, no problem. I want you to pay me back in a few months. However, if you like, I can introduce you to a gentleman who can help you be successful in your business.

"Thank you, but who is he?" said my father.

Mr. Sau immediately said, "The Lord Jesus Christ."

He began telling my father about God's love and salvation. In response to Mr. Sau's evangelism, my father accepted the Lord Jesus Christ as his personal Savior. My father came home with some Vietnamese evangelistic tracts and put them in the roof of our boat, which was made of coconut leaves. No one in our family knew my father had converted from Buddhism to Christianity until my older brother Kiet found those small books on the boat roof and shouted, "Dad became a Christian!"

Hearing my brother say so, my mother was so upset that she shouted, "Why! Why!" She began arguing against my father, saying, "Why did you change your religion without saying even one word to me? Do you know my father was a strong Buddhist, and if he was still alive, he would be very angry?"

My father did not understand much about Christianity, so he just sat still, saying, "I am sorry! Mr. Sau said that the Lord Jesus Christ could help me to run my small business because He is so powerful. I am very embarrassed, as I accepted his invitation without one word of refusal. If you want me to come back to our traditional religion, I will do so to please you for our family harmony."

My mother did not argue anymore with my father until three days after the argument. My mother then said to my father, "Can you take me to your church?"

My father was surprised and asked, "Why? Please do not cause any problems toward the church. The church did not do anything wrong toward us. I beg you, please."

My mother smiled and said, "No, I will not do anything against the church, but I would like to follow your Lord as you did some days ago."

My father sincerely asked my mother, "Really?"

"Yes, I want to follow the Lord Jesus Christ." My mother then told my father and the whole family about her nightmare the previous night. In it she had met a demon with a terrible face who was speaking terrible words. He chased her on a very long road but did not catch her until she saw a church. Some people who were standing in the church's front yard were happily laughing and talking to my mother, saying, "Do not run anymore. Just come in here. The demon will not catch you in here, because our dear Lord Jesus Christ protects us from any demons. He does not allow any demons to stay in His church."

My mother asked them, "But how can I come into your church when the gate is closed?" All the church members stretched to catch my mother's hand and pull her onto the front yard. When my mother stayed on the front yard of the church, the demon shouted loudly and ran away from her.

Everybody said, "Hallelujah! Amen!"

My mother was peaceful in the churchyard with the church members. On waking up, my mother said to herself that the Lord Jesus Christ, whom my father trusted, was the true and powerful Spirit. The next morning, she went to church with all her children to hear the pastor's prayers because she believed in the Lord Jesus Christ. The whole family together trusted in the Lord Jesus Christ after that and received baptism performed by Rev. Hien Van Le from Can Tho, about sixty kilometers north of Soc Trang, in 1947, when I was eight years old.

Although I was still young, I knew the meaning of salvation. From the beginning, mankind's ancestors disobeyed God but obeyed Satan by eating "from the tree of which I commanded you not to eat" (Genesis 3:11). They sinned against the Lord and received the consequences, such as toiling for a living, pain in childbirth, and death. The Bible explains why mankind's ancestral sin became all men's sin: "Therefore, just as through one man sin entered into the world, and death through sin, and so death spread to all men, because all sinned" (Romans 5:12). Man was unable to save himself, but God's only begotten Son acted as a sacrifice to save all mankind by His death on the cross, which the Bible describes as follows: "By this the love of God was manifested in us, that God has sent His only begotten Son into the world so that we might live through Him. In this is love, not that we loved God, but that He loved us and sent His Son to be the propitiation for our sins" (1 John 4:9–10). The Lord Jesus Christ did His part: death on the cross. We must do our part: accept His sacrifice for each of us and believe in Him as our personal Savior.

Since I became the Lord's child, I embraced the Bible as my treasure, my most precious possession, by reading every day, memorizing some important passages and key verses for my spiritual life. I seldom missed even one Sunday worship service. I attended Children's Sunday school and joined the children's choir to praise the Lord in any church holiday services. I sat on the front bench, close to the pulpit, to hear the preacher's sermon clearly. I even retold it to some people who missed a Sunday.

I visited my Christian friends who were absent from the Sunday school class or the church services. I recited the Bible passages to say that as a little child of Christ, I loved every man. Remember that the Lord says, "I DESIRE COMPASSION, AND NOT A SACRIFICE" (Matthew 12:7). Sacrifice belongs to the law, but compassion belongs to the heart. Remember: the first nature of the fruit of the Holy Spirit is love. (See Galatians 5:22.) The passage of love in 1 Corinthians 13:1–13 is the most important passage of the Bible. Christianity's emphasis is love!

In Christ's love, I needed to be tested. I learned from my Sunday school teacher that God gave His children some tests—not to know them but to help them grow spiritually. Even Abraham, Israel's patriarch, was also tested at least three times in his earthly life. His first test was to leave his homeland to become the ancestor of Israel's people. He easily passed this test. The second was his faith in the Lord about a son whom his wife Sarah herself gave birth to. He failed this test because he pleased his wife instead by marrying a second wife, Hagar, and having a son, Ismael. This was not God's will. The third test was the offering of his son Isaac, his son with Sarah, as a burnt sacrifice at Mount Moriah. The Bible's description of this tough test is as follows: "By faith Abraham, when he was tested, offered up Isaac, and he who had received the promises was offering up his only begotten son; it was he to whom it was said, 'IN ISAAC YOUR DESCENDANTS SHALL BE CALLED'" (Hebrews 11:17–18).

As the Lord's child, even still in my boyhood, I was tested at least twice. The first test came in the form of smallpox that covered my body before my first Christmas. At the Christmas service in 1947, I was assigned to recite a ten-verse poem that I had memorized about the Lord's birth. I had already memorized the whole poem when I came down with smallpox. I endured the disease in silence until the Christmas celebration was over.

The second test came from the loss of a prized possession—a pen I was given in 1948 when I completed the highest grade in school. One day the students from our school got together at Soc Trang Airport to welcome King Bao Dai. We arrived on time, with a few moments for rest. When I reached into my pocket, I discovered that my pen was no longer there. My sadness was so great that I cried at the loss. However, I remembered the Lord's power and will, and I prayed that I would be able to forget my precious possession. I forgot it easily and passed the test. Since those experiences from my boyhood when I have encountered suffering, I have often applied the same methods: prayer, trust, and obedience.

My Occupation

My favorite Biblical passage is 1 Corinthians 13; the key verse is John 3:16, and a key person is Joseph (Jacob's son, Isaac's grandson, noted in the book of Genesis chapters 37 to 50). Joseph is the typical Biblical saint in my opinion, even though you don't see him described as Noah was: "But Noah found favor in the eyes of the LORD" (Genesis 6:8). Yet "Joseph found favor in his sight" (Genesis 39:4). "His sight" refers not to the Lord but rather to Potiphar of Egypt

However, "The LORD was with Joseph, so he became a successful man" (Genesis 39:2). I read through Joseph's life in Genesis and agree with this Scripture and the other happenings: (1) he did not blame his brothers for throwing him into the pit and later selling him to the Ishmaelites to be a slave; (2) he did not blame Potiphar's wife for falsely accusing him, causing him to be imprisoned; and (3) he did not avenge his brothers for what they did to him. Through these actions, I learned about Joseph's heartfelt gratitude and love for his father and brothers.

Joseph did not do great things, as did many of the well-known prophets and apostles in Scripture. He did ordinary things, but sometimes even ordinary things are hard for common people to accomplish. It is hard to love and forgive an enemy, even those who are blood brothers and sisters. It is hard to pay tribute to those who mistreat us. But Joseph was able to do what the Bible says, and he had no biblical instructions in his time.

Following Joseph's example of showing gratitude to his parents, I prayed and imitated that gratitude so that I might be a good son to my parents. The best way I could accomplish that was to be diligent in my education. I tried my best to pass the vocational school tests to be selected for admission.

The National Commerce School needed sixty students, but 1,200 applications were sent to the school. Those accepted would be required to attend three consecutive years at school. Graduates of the school would be appointed to work as provincial directors of economy, taxation, finance, or treasuries. The National Pedagogy School needed three hundred students, but there were three thousand applicants. Those who were selected would study at the school just one year. Graduates would be appointed as public elementary school teachers. The salary a graduate could obtain was quite different between the two schools, with a National Pedagogy School graduate having a salary far less than a National Commerce School graduate.

By God's grace, I was selected by both schools based on my examination. The National Commerce School's examination results were posted first, so I chose to attend there. Once the National Pedagogy School posted the results and I saw I had been accepted, I realized I had a choice.

I prayed for God's will. God told me to pick the teaching career in spite of its lower salary. I really did not know why God's will for me was teaching rather than administration, accounting, or business. It wasn't until I was drafted into the army, and especially when I entered into Christian ministry in the United States, that I understood.

Hearing my quick decision to switch from commerce to pedagogy, my commerce school classmates were upset, and they came to see me immediately. One of them asked, "Are you crazy, Minh?"

The other said, "You are so stupid. You made a bad choice. Just compare the salaries of the two occupations; you will see a big difference. As an elementary school teacher, you will be teaching in the small village, but you could work in the big city as a director of the governmental office."

I kept silent, just smiled, and said, "Thank you for your concerns and counseling, friends. But I think I have made the right choice. I believe God knows my destiny. I hope we still have the opportunity to see each other again, despite our different schools." They looked so sad, and all together they stood up, said good-bye to me, and left.

I began my teaching career in September 1959 in the Soc Trang province when I was twenty years old. I taught the fifth grade at Vinh Quoi Elementary School, then Thanh Phu School. The schools were located beside the national route between the two provinces of Soc Trang and Bac-lieu, which allowed me to take the passenger bus to school and back home every day. The school was far from the center of Soc Trang province—about eighteen kilometers, which took fifteen minutes to drive.

After just a few months of teaching fifth grade, I was promoted to school principal. This was so strange to me, because I became a principal at the age of just twenty-one years old; I was very young and lacking in experience. Once I saw the school superintendent's letter, I realized that I was the only teacher on staff, as the others were supernumerary and thus unqualified to take such a position.

One day the principal of Truong Khanh Elementary School came to my house and asked me to switch schools with him. He wanted to work at my school so he could look after land he owned near the school. The switch worked in my favor as well, as it brought me closer to my parents' house. We both signed an agreement to switch schools, and I started there during the following school year in 1960.

My whole salary was given to my parents, just as I wished. I was so satisfied because the prayers I had said since childhood had been accepted. What did I pray to the Lord? I prayed that the Lord would give me good health so that I could study hard and reach my educational goals. I prayed that I would live until I turned eighteen and could work to earn some money. I planned to give my parents all the money I earned. The Lord accepted my request, and I was able to show my gratitude to my parents, just as Joseph did to his father.

My teaching career was good; many of my fifth-grade students passed the test to be selected for admission at the public middle and high school without tuition. The students' parents were very happy because they did not spend money for their children's tuition for seven consecutive years, from the sixth grade to the senior year.

I believed God helped me find a job that was suitable for my health, ability, and skill level. My school was near my parents' house and my local church, so I could attend worship service and Sunday school every Sunday, and also join some church activities with my close friends and relatives. Praise the Lord for answering my prayers and giving me the teaching job. I was so thankful to the Lord for the success in my profession. Hallelujah! Amen!

My Marriage

I did not intend to marry when I was still very young, as I just wanted to continue my unfinished education. At the time, I had a good job and income, but I had not completed high school yet. My father and the father of a kindergarten teacher next door had discussed and agreed that his daughter and I would enter into an arranged marriage. They made this agreement without speaking to either of us but said they would speak to us later and hoped we would agree.

She and I only ever spoke when she came to our house for groceries, as my mother turned the front of our home into a small grocery store for the neighbors. My father and I seldom discussed the topic of my marriage, but one day the young woman came to our home with a bowl of vegetable soup in her hands. Taking advantage of that situation, my father asked her "Whom do you want to give the bowl of soup to, Anh?"

She bashfully answered my father's question: "To uncle Anh."

"Why do you give it to uncle Anh?" my father asked.

She answered, "He and I have the same name."

Anh was my youngest brother, who had the same first name as she did. After she left us, my father said to me, "You need to marry her. If you two became spouses, your salaries would double. In case you join the army and are wounded in action, her salary could help. That is the advantage of marriage."

I did not like to argue with my father about marriage. However, I was concerned about the difference in our beliefs, as she was a strong Catholic and I was interested in the evangelical doctrine. I was afraid of future disagreements, quarrelling, and troubles between husband and wife. I just said to my father, "I think it is difficult; she is a Catholic, and I am a Protestant."

My father seemed to be angry, saying, "Both Catholics and Protestants worship the same Lord, no difference."

I did not discuss it anymore with my father, who had already promised the marriage to her father. I kept silent and prayed. I talked to the Lord about my plan of education and asked Him about my marriage, "Lord, who will be my wife—Miss Anh, my neighbor, as my father wills, or someone else? I really need your help."

My father and I did not discuss the matter of my marriage for about a year. I think perhaps the subject wasn't interesting to my father because the decision had already been made.

One day, I stopped by Mr. Hoa's house for church business. Mr. Hoa was an elected deacon chair of my church and was Khanh's older brother. Khanh later became my wife. The heavy rain outside seemed to keep me in the house longer than expected. Taking advantage of this, he asked me, "Aren't you married?"

I promptly answered him, "No."

"Why?" he asked.

I answered, "I am still very young, and I have not completed my basic education yet."

He said, "I think it is enough. You have a very good salary. You see many soldiers that have a small salary but a big family, and they survived easily. God cares for them."

I answered, "Whom should I marry, do you think?"

Without hesitation, he said to me, "My younger sister Khanh."

I knew Khanh well because we had been classmates in the church school where her father and Mr. Hoa taught the church members' children during the war between Viet Minh and the French army in 1947. I did not know if Khanh liked me, because she often went upstairs whenever I came to visit her parents' family during my stay in Saigon for two years. So I said, "I do not know if she likes me."

Mr. Hoa said, "I will ask my sister Hiep to go to Saigon. She will ask Khanh about marriage. I hope for no problems at all. Just wait and see!" The next day, her sister Hiep came from Soc Trang to talk to Khanh in Saigon about marriage.

Hiep said, "Khanh, come here. Let's talk about your marriage."

Khanh was so bashful when first hearing about her marriage, so she asked, "What?"

"Your marriage," Hiep said.

"With whom?"

"Teacher Minh."

When she heard "Teacher Minh," she felt a little surprised and thrilled, and she said, "What teacher Minh?"

Hiep said, "Son of Mr. Cam—you know. He is our church member in Soc Trang. Do you know him?"

Khanh now became bold and said, "Yes, I know him."

"He asked to marry you. Do you agree?"

Without hesitation, she immediately answered Hiep, "Yes. I do."

Hiep was a little disappointed, thinking that Khanh was kidding and did not want to marry me. She slowly explained, "Khanh. Be careful. This is an important and very serious matter. I do not want you to ignore this. I am too busy with my current business down there, you know. I spent two days just for this matter. I do not want you to be kidding. Tell me the truth. Do you want to marry Minh?"

Khanh was very honest and never ignored the important matter. She especially respected her oldest sister Hiep. She said, "Oh no! I dare not kid or lie to you, sister. I'm telling you that I would like to marry Teacher Minh."

"Do you love him?" Hiep said.

"Yes," Khanh answered.

"If this is true, try to go to Soc Trang and talk to him someday."

Khanh said, "Yes. When I finish some stuff here, then I will go to Soc Trang."

Some days later, Khanh went to Soc Trang to meet with me at Mr. Hoa's house. I asked her if she loved me, and she said yes.

"When did you know?" I asked

"When you came to stay at my house for a rest during your study at the National Pedagogy School."

"But why did you go upstairs when I came to your house purposely to talk to you?"

"I was bashful," she said.

"Oh, you and I love each other. I wanted to talk to you about our future marriage after my graduation from the pedagogy school, but you always seemed to hide from me. I thought you did not like me, because you did not want to see me. If your brother had not asked me about marriage, we would have never cleared up this misunderstanding. You really love me but did not want me to see you. Love should be expressed by genuine words and actions, quite different from your way. But praise the Lord for today's meeting and understanding among us. I really love you, Khanh. And I need you to confirm your decision now by your own statement."

"Yes, Minh, I do love you. This is why I came down here to meet with you for a discussion of our future marriage. Praise the Lord for this meeting and God's will for both of us to unite in a Christian marriage."

The two of us had dinner before leaving that place and talked of meeting again the following day. That night I was so impressed, thinking of the rainy day when I had a conversation about marriage with Mr. Hoa. Mr. Hoa purposely wanted me to marry his younger sister Khanh; she loved me, and I had truly loved her ever since I went to Saigon for my education. But we had never before met and expressed our love to each other.

I had to ride on my bicycle from Gia Dinh to the National Pedagogy School five days a week to study for the whole day in both a morning and an afternoon class. One time I was sick and needed a rest between the two class sessions. I asked my mother to beg Khanh's parents to allow me to stay at her house for two hours of rest before going back to school for the afternoon class. Her family joyfully accepted my mother's request, and Khanh also cooked a good lunch for me to take every day. After I was married, she told me that she had saved her own money to make those delicious meals for me. Her sincere words made me so happy. I believed that God loved me and helped me in my marriage by providing me with a very spiritual Christian woman who really loved her husband and shared all her precious treasures with him.

She depended on me for everything in our future marriage. Her needs were simple, and she did not need me to spend money for a dress, shoes, or jewelry for the wedding. We took time to meet with each other, borrowing an Italian motorbike from my adopted brother, Chao, to venture around the city so that she could see the landscape of Soc Trang.

I solemnly promised her that I would not change my mind about this marriage. In case there were any problems with my parents, I said I would never marry any other girl. She, likewise, would never marry another man. We prayed a lot for our marriage.

In actuality, a problem came from my sister, as she and Khanh's older sister had a long-standing quarrel over church uniforms. My sister got upset when she heard of my marriage to Khanh. However, she confessed later that she had misunderstood Khanh, who did not present herself the way my sister once thought.

On Saturday, October 28, 1961, both of our parents met to discuss the wedding. Khanh stayed at my parents' house to live with me. I went to work at Khanh's school, Truong, every day except Saturday and Sunday.

Dr. and Mrs. Minh Van Lam.

Chapter 8

The Second Miracle: What a Strange Birth

A Difficult Delivery

Khanh was pregnant and going to give birth. At 8:00 p.m. on September 12, 1962, in Soc Trang, she felt the painful symptoms of childbirth begin, and so an older woman accompanied her to the private maternity hospital by pedicab. The older woman returned about an hour later with a look of embarrassment upon her face. She said that Khanh had been bleeding since she arrived at the hospital and so the hospital director did not want to risk admitting her to their hospital. She needed more care than they could provide.

When I arrived with my adopted brother in his car, we took Khanh very quickly to the main public hospital, where doctors and nurses worked as professionals trained by the government medical school in Saigon. Khanh was too weak to deliver, as she had already lost too much blood. The nurse called the doctor, who was sleeping at home. Khanh miserably screamed out, calling upon the Lord and her mother. I kept praying with her brother outside the delivery room. The nurse went out to meet us and said, "She kept calling to the Lord and her mother very pitifully. The doctor has been called and will be coming here pretty soon."

I prayed to the Lord, remembering the key verse of prayer in an emergency, Jeremiah 33:3: "Call to Me, and I will answer you, and I will tell you great and mighty things, which you do not know." I heard the nurse's voice: "The doctor wants to perform surgery just to save the mother, and we cannot keep the baby. But unfortunately there is not enough available type O blood, which is the mother's blood type. The mother should be transported to Can Tho hospital to get additional type O blood." I intended to ask my adopted brother to drive his car so my wife could undergo this surgery in Can Tho, about sixty kilometers from Soc Trang. But we did not know whether she would be able to hold on that long.

While everybody was discussing how we would transport my wife to Can Tho an hour later, my adopted brother said, "No, we do not need to go to Can Tho for type O blood, as my blood type is O; I could donate my blood to her." Everyone was so glad! The doctor checked his blood and said it was a little bit low. However, it would be okay for the surgery.

When everything was ready for surgery, the doctor suddenly thought of another method to deliver the baby without surgery. He felt the baby turn its head in the direction necessary to slowly remove the baby. From that point, it was easy for him to pull the baby's head out of the mother's womb using pincers. Little by little, he slowly pulled the baby's head until he successfully finished the tough job of delivering the child. He loudly announced, "Both the mother and the girl are alive!" At that time, we didn't have ultrasounds to tell us the gender of the baby, so that was the first we knew it was a girl.

The baby did not cry upon delivery, because she was too weak. The doctor repeatedly rubbed the baby as though he were washing a bath basin, and finally he felt her breath. He handed the baby to the chief nurse, and we all expressed our appreciation to both the doctor and the chief nurse for their work.

My wife and my daughter became increasingly weak. My wife was too weak to speak even one word, and our daughter was too weak to cry one sound. The nurses surrounded the baby with two hot water bottles to keep her warm over several days. Minh Phuong was the name we gave our daughter, who was born on the thirteenth of September 1962.

Nobody believed that both the mother and the baby could survive such an ordeal. If Khanh had been taken to Can Tho by my adopted brother for surgery, she probably would have died from exhaustion. We did not know my adopted brother's blood type was O, and we had no other way to solve this big problem.

Jeremiah 33:3 was the phone number I used to call God's office. The Lord was available to pick up the phone and immediately answer, ensuring that both mother and daughter would be okay She is now fifty-two years old and married with two daughters, living in the city of Fort Smith, Arkansas. She serves the Lord as the children's Sunday school teacher and church soloist.

Praise the Lord for God's miracle, which saved my wife and my daughter. We will never forget that during a horrible night, the Lord suddenly presented a volunteer blood donor and the doctor switched the delivery method and used pincers to save both my wife and daughter.

Reverend Dr. Minh Van Lam

Mrs. Minh Van Lam.

A Deadly Disease

In 1964, when Minh Phuong was two years old, she got a serious disease that almost killed her. She could not eat or sleep, and her skin became increasingly dark. She was very skinny, could not open her eyes, and could not sit up. Some doctors came to examine her and gave her medication, but it was in vain. We were depressed and thought she would gradually get weaker until she died. I prayed to the Lord, asking Him to heal her: "Oh dear Lord, she might have died in her mother's womb before delivery, but you saved her life. Now she is in danger. Please come to help us from this terrible and miserable problem!"

Everyone who came to visit her would look at her body and shake his or her head in disappointment. We did nothing other than pray and remember her miraculous birth at the hospital, trusting that the Lord could also heal her fatal disease.

God's miracle truly happened. Minh Phuong naturally felt better and better until she was fully recovered and healthy. We praised the Lord for His love and healing, offering her to the Lord for His use when she grew into adulthood. She was an active daughter; she helped my wife do the errands, looking after her younger sisters and brother while I was imprisoned in the reeducation camps. After I was released from prison, she left us to work as a maid in Saigon and sent money to our family to help with some financial problems. She is now working at her own salon and nail business.

After her birth, my wife gave birth to three other children: our second daughter, Phuong Loan, in 1964; our only son, Duy Ai, in 1971; and our youngest daughter, Thuy Linh, in 1973. Loan works at the food service department of a public elementary school in Austin, Texas; her husband, Tuyen Nguyen, works for IBM and is a bivocational pastor of the Vietnamese United Baptist Church in Austin, Texas. Our only son, Duy Ai, works as the pianist for a Methodist church in Morrow Bay, California; his wife, Uyen Phuong, works for a post office in Morrow Bay. Our youngest daughter, Thuy Linh, and her husband work as civil servants for the government. Phuong has two daughters, Loan has one daughter and one son, Ai has one daughter, and Linh has five sons. Therefore, my wife and I have ten grandchildren.

We have been living in harmony for over fifty-three years with four years of separation because of military training, overseas English training, and reeducation in the Communist camps. We are thankful to the Lord, who helped unite Khanh Minh Ngo and Minh Van Lam in a Christian marriage with so many blessings. Hallelujah! Amen!

Chapter 9

The Third Miracle: Missed a Bomb Explosion

When I started going to my elementary school in Vinh Chau village, I studied French in the second grade as a second-language requirement. In addition to Vietnamese, I also studied British English in middle school and high school.

French was hard to write, and English was hard to speak. French grammar was difficult, as was English pronunciation. As a high school student, I had to take two foreign language courses every school year. I was able to write in French and English, but I could not speak the languages.

After my wedding in 1961, I planned to learn to speak English with some GIs who rented my father's rooms, as their facilities were close by and security was not an issue. I boldly spoke English with some friendly American soldiers whose sweethearts were Vietnamese girls. Before starting my self-study program, I knelt down and prayed, "My dear heavenly Father, because of the Tower of Babel, constructed by the rebels after the world flood during Noah's time, you created many different languages. (See Genesis 11:7.) I now beg you to give me just one international language—English. I will use my knowledge of this international language for serving you in the future. I am so thankful to you. I pray in the name of the Lord, Jesus Christ. Amen!" (See Acts 2:4.)

I bought a pocket radio to listen to the English program *Dictation from Vietnam*, which was read by a Vietnamese woman on a Saigon radio station every night. Thanks to the daily self-study at home, my English was progressively improving little by little. I kept learning English day and night until I was able to speak with those soldiers that stayed in my father's house. I soon felt that my English was good enough for me to take the baccalaureate, which I had failed four times while I was still a high school student.

I went with my relative from Soc Trang to Can Tho to show that I passed the first baccalaureate. On the way back to Soc Trang, we were standing by the road, waiting for the bus. When it came to the bus stop, I was about to get on it, but suddenly my relative told me to wait while he used the toilet. The bus could not wait, so it left. When he was finished, we had to wait for another bus. I blamed him for the two additional hours we had to wait for another bus.

Two hours later, another bus came, and we boarded the bus. On the way home, the bus driver made a complete stop; this surprised every passenger. They asked him, "Why did you stop?"

He said loudly, "Do you see a big pillar of black smoke in front of us? I do not know what happened. Let's go forward to see it. I'm guessing a bomb exploded!"

Indeed, as we approached, we saw a bus full of dead bodies, some of which had been thrown on the road. Almost everyone was dead, with the exception of the driver, who was seriously wounded. My relative said to me, "You see, we escaped death. If I had not gone to the toilet, we would not be alive. I believe God loves us and wanted us to be alive." I think of my relative's notion and silently praise the Lord for the miracle that saved our lives.

After arriving home, we told our family members about the mysterious event of the bomb explosion and the many victims we had seen. They were all frightened but were thankful to the Lord for His care and protection from this horrible danger.

I began studying to take the second baccalaureate examination. I mailed a copy of the certificate of the first baccalaureate to the army recruitment office according to the Department of Defense's order. One month later, I received the call-up papers from the Army Recruiting Department, which commanded me to report to the provincial military headquarters on March 25, 1965, to join the army and receive military training at Thu Duc Military Academy. Both my self-study toward continuous education and my teaching career were interrupted.

I kept silent, thinking of God's will. My prayers for the opportunity to self-study English seemed rejected by the Lord. I really loved teaching, and it seemed like the right choice. Why had the Lord given me a snake instead of a fish, a scorpion instead of an egg? (See Luke 11:11–12.) I remembered some verses I had memorized for sad cases like this: "Be anxious for nothing, but in everything by prayer and supplication with thanksgiving let your requests be made known to God. And the peace of God, which surpasses all comprehension, will guard your hearts and your minds in Christ Jesus" (Philippians 4:6–7). God's will was quite different from man's will, "'For My thoughts are not your thoughts, nor are your ways My ways' declares the LORD. 'For as the heavens are higher than the earth, So are My ways higher than your ways, and My thoughts than your thoughts'" (Isaiah 55:8–9).

I had to be ready and prepared for a future in the military. I had to leave my school, my church, and my family—including my parents, brothers, sisters, wife, and two daughters—for the military service. I had to wait and see what happened to my family and me.

I expected a blessing from the Lord, just as Jacob encountered on the way to his mother's hometown, as described in Genesis 28:10–22. I also expected to hear from the Lord in the same way He had talked to Jacob: "Behold, I am with you and will keep you wherever you go, and will bring you back to this land; for I will not leave you until I have done what I have promised you" (Genesis 28:15).

To me, the dark sky became darker, covering all the scenes on the earth like an announcement of the dark days upon the whole world. This made my heart hurt, as I was leaving relatives for battle without knowing whether I would survive or not. It was like Jacob's circumstance after leaving Beersheba. He came to a place on the way to Haran, and he spent the night there, using one stone as a pillow for sleeping. Thinking of the future, he might depend on only the Lord for help and guidance. (See Genesis 28:10–17.) It seems to me that both Jacob and Joseph gave me good examples to live by during the separation from my parents and family. I talked to the Lord very often, day and night, so that I could be close to Him while I could not be close to my relatives.

I was not familiar with military service and was not interested in it either. My occupation was teaching kids, and now I was going to reluctantly join the army to fight and to work in dangerous situations, with military discipline and the anxiety that comes with battle. In addition to looking to Jacob and Joseph as pioneers for acquiring peace, I used David's poem in this new stage of life: "Even though I walk through the valley of the shadow of death, I fear no evil, for You are with me; Your rod and Your staff, they comfort me" (Psalm 23:4).

Section III
God's Miracles for My Military Service

Chapter 10

The Fourth Miracle: God's Response to My Prayer

The Army Medical Doctor Says, "No, I can't!"

All the men with call-up papers had to report to the provincial military headquarters for transportation to Can Tho for medical examination. A military GMC bus without a roof transported five young men to the large city. We didn't speak a single word during the trip, as we were all thinking of the family and friends we had left. We were missing them and imagining the upcoming hardships we might experience at the academy.

I continued to think of my family and prayed that the Lord would protect them from suffering in my absence. I believed my wife could handle small family problems or sick children, but I prayed that the Lord would be with them day and night and bring support from our relatives.

It took us about an hour to get to Can Tho, and we were shocked to see crowds of young men in the camp. All of these young men had to obey the government orders to join up during the civil war between the North Vietnamese and South Vietnamese armed forces.

The next day, we were all prepared for our medical examination. I arrived at the last section and awaited the results of the exam. The doctor had a vacant stare and said, "If your weight were lower just one point, you might be free from military service."

His words made me joyful. I was insistent and said, "So please, allow me to be free; I appreciate your courtesy and help. I am an elementary school teacher, often unhealthy and sick, and I have a family with two children to care for. Would you please have mercy and compassion for my family?" I kept begging, but unfortunately he refused to help.

He then said, "Can you hold a revolver, a pistol? It is the lightest gun for an officer to hold. You do not have to carry a heavy gun."

I tried again to ask him for help. "My wife and children really need me. Without me, they will suffer."

He responded, "No, I am not allowed to show favor to you, as I am responsible for all military personnel. If I show favor to you, I have to show favor to the others, and then I will not have enough officers to provide for the army. Prepare for the trip to Thu Duc Military Academy tomorrow. I hope to see you again as an army officer, not as a civilian.

I was frustrated, thinking *Is this God's will for me—to fight in battle instead of teaching children at a peaceful elementary school?* If God did not want me to fight against other humans, he would have commanded the medical doctor to reduce my weight by the one point I needed. I would have been free that day to go home to my family. Why did God want me to join the army during this war? It was pretty hard for me to answer that question then, but just wait and see!

The Chaplain Says, "I won't preach!"

Those who passed the physical examinations were taken to Thu Duc Military Academy. This was the largest training academy for reserve army officers. My class was named the Twentieth and consisted of 1,500 cadets.

The military training was composed of two phases, with each phase lasting four months. After two months of basic training, a cadet received the Alpha Sign. If a cadet did not earn the Alpha Sign, he or she could not leave the military facilities for any reason. One night in the barracks, we heard an announcement made by a Vietnamese Evangelical Church chaplain, who typically preached at 9:00 a.m. every Sunday. The following day was the first Sunday of military worship for the new cadets who were Protestant. I went to the worship service to hear the chaplain, Captain Thai Van Nguyen, preach.

I was surprised when I got there, as Captain Thai was the only one there. He looked upset and asked me, "How about the other Christians? This is the list of the cadets, the Evangelical Church Christians, I got from the joint general staff. There are twenty-seven Christians; only one of you came?"

I said, "I really don't know, Captain. Nobody told me about the current number of Christians in this military school."

A few minutes later, another cadet named Thu arrived. After talking to us for a while, the chaplain said, "I want one of you to run around the school buildings, to each company, every Saturday afternoon to remind the Christian cadets of the Sunday worship service here. Which one of you wants to announce this to the companies?" I immediately raised my hand and said yes. He handed me a piece of paper on which was a list of the current Christian cadets. The chaplain finally said with a sad feeling, "I won't preach today, because there are only two of you, but next Sunday I will. Let me pray for you." After his prayers, he left us.

I didn't know why these twenty-five other cadets wouldn't want to attend worship and seek the Lord's protection when they were far away from family and in military training. The second

Sunday arrived, and I met the chaplain and his driver again at 9:00 a.m. He immediately asked, "Minh, did you go to each company to invite the cadets to come here today for the worship service?"

I replied, "Yes, Captain. I met each of them at their companies, telling them about you and the worship service. I do not know why no one has come, since it is 9:00 a.m. now."

The chaplain seemed very sad. He looked at his watch, shook his head, and said "Two men came last Sunday; I thought some more would come here today, but only you have come. I will report to the joint general staff that most of the cadets do not want to attend the worship service and I do not need to preach to just one Christian! I will pray for you and leave. What do you want me to pray about, Minh?

"I need your prayers for my safety during military training, prayers for my wife and two little daughters in Saigon, and most importantly that my future is not in battle, as I am most unskillful in fighting and would like to be an elementary school teacher again one day.

My requests touched the chaplain's heart. He prayed for me: "Oh our dear Lord, I believe Minh is your faithful Christian, because he came here for worship service every Sunday morning. Protect him from any danger during his training here. Give him a safe place to serve the country after his graduation from this military academy. Bless his family, his wife, and his little children in Saigon. I pray in the name of the Lord, Jesus Christ. Amen!"

Shaking my hand, the chaplain and his driver said good-bye and left me. He never came back to see me again at the military school, partly because I was allowed to visit home in Saigon after I received the Alpha Sign.

Whenever I left the barracks to visit home, I worshiped with my family at Ban Co Vietnamese Evangelical Church, which is located on Phan Thanh Gian Street, in front of the Binh Dan Hospital. I never missed a single service during the eight months of military training. I always remembered to pray for my future military service. In addition to the prayers at church and at home, I prayed every day during times of rest and even during the tough training activities, such as climbing the mountain, swimming, taking a potentially fatal zip line through a little valley, fighting in the mud in the jungle, and taking lessons in the classroom and the weapon ranges.

The platoon leader cadre selected me to be the cadet leader, who commands the whole company during a platoon's turn to present the class to the trainer prior to his teaching. Each trainer gave the highest grade to our company every time I acted as the company leader. This excellent presentation with strict discipline and military order gave the trainer a good impression of our company, and we were rated the best company of all. The award for this evaluation was two consecutive days off during the weekend for all the cadets of our company to visit home. As for me, my platoon cadre said that I was given the highest score for good conduct, which contributed to our final grade toward graduation and unit assignment.

After four months, the first part of the training was over. The cadets were classified as professional officers and were set to move on to other professional schools for training. Half of the cadets stayed at Thu Duc to be trained as army officers. I did not move on to another professional military school; I stayed at Thu Duc Military Academy to be trained as a professional fighter for battle.

That night I could not sleep, thinking of my poor family. My destiny was to fight in battle. In four short months, I would be appointed as platoon leader to an army division that would fight against another hostile unit. I figured I would die or become wounded and unhelpfully handicapped, only to burden my wife and children. A dark curtain seemed to cover my eyes, and I could not see a bright future—only the dark storms ahead. My platoon leader, Lieutenant Men Van Mai, who used to be a schoolteacher like me, saw my sadness and said, "I have seen your sorrow these days. What made you sad? Does your stay here make you disappointed?"

"Yes, Lieutenant" I replied. "I have a family to care for. If I have to fight, and die, how can they live without me?"

"Don't worry. I will help you to work at a military academy. You don't have to fight."

In spite of Lieutenant Men's comfort, I was still worried a great deal. I did not depend on men, but just the Lord. I kept praying, "Oh Lord, I now know my future. I will fight because I am at Thu Duc Military Academy to be trained as an army officer. Have you forgotten me? Do you want to see me die? Do you want to see me live far from my family? Oh Lord, save me from this deadly situation. I know you are powerful and have mercy and compassion. Take pity on my family and me. I have only one you to depend on and to hope for. Do not leave me, Lord."

I prayed that way every day until one day that I now call the day of God's miracle. I mysteriously changed from sorrow to joy, from frustration to hope, from death to survival, and from anxiety to peace. It was unbelievable, and impossible to imagine. It was a great blessing that could come only from heaven. It happened almost fifty years ago, but to me it seemed as if it were only yesterday.

An English Test

For a brief period of time, I still needed to repeat my prayer. I prayed at home in Soc Trang, at the recruiting office in Can Tho, at Thu Duc Military Academy every morning after I got up, every noon at lunch, during every class at school, out in the jungle, and every evening before I went to bed. I asked my relatives, my chaplain, my Christian friends, and anybody I knew to pray for me. Unfortunately I was not selected for a nice branch that would allow me to stay at the rear; I had to fight at the front. I dropped down moment by moment like an animal falling down from a high tree to the ground. I grew more and more pessimistic, thinking of life as a tragedy with a tragic beginning and a miserable end.

I was genuinely surprised that the Lord did not hear my prayers. I read the Bible, so I knew the stories of the saints and the tests and miracles that only the almighty God could do for those that faithfully trusted Him. Hannah's prayers were heard, and she gave birth to her son, Samuel. King Hezekiah's prayers were heard, and his disease was healed. I prayed, so why were my prayers not heard, and why did I keep staying in this academy to die in an infantry battle? I knew the Bible well, but when I encountered some tests and problems that I felt I could not endure, I gave up. The Lord wanted me to see His power, and He wanted to see my patience so that I had to learn from Him and see His miracles.

One night the company leader read an announcement about an English test that would take place the following day for those with a good knowledge of English, as they were looking for instructors at the Armed Forces Language School in Saigon. The announcement encouraged the talented English teachers, interpreters, and the American agency employees because they had used English in their careers. I ignored it, because I felt my English was not good enough for a competition with professional English speakers and writers. The English test passed by silently without my participation.

The next month, another announcement from the same school was read about an English test for those who would like to work as liaison officers with the Allied Forces. The Allied Forces consisted of the United States, Thailand, the Philippines, and Australia. I ignored this announcement too. The cadets named infantrymen by the trainers had two more months of training until graduation.

The last announcement for an English test was made for liaison officers to the Korean division. I don't know why I paid very close attention to the announcement; perhaps it was because Koreans were Asians, like the Vietnamese. After the meeting, I asked the announcement reader to let me see the copy of the announcement. I read over it and decided to register for the test.

I prayed before I went to take the test. There were 120 candidates who competed to work with Korean soldiers. I did not know the number of candidates that were to be selected. The test consisted of one hundred questions; half of it was read aloud by a civilian American, and the other half contained questions on grammar. It took an hour to finish the tough test.

I did not worry so much about the results, because I wasn't aware of how many liaisons were required. I just waited for God's will. Tuesday night was important to those of us who took the test on Monday, as the administrators were set to make an announcement regarding the oral test we had to take on Wednesday. The announcement was read, and everyone stood still to hear who would take the oral test.

I was so surprised and thrilled when I heard my full name read as the fifth candidate to be selected for an oral test. Two examiners gave the test. I was called to step forward and sit beside an American civilian for an interview. He asked me, smiling, "What are you going to do this afternoon after the test?"

I was able to understand his question and answered him immediately. "Sir, I will study the Howitzer 3.5 this afternoon."

He nodded as a sign of approval and asked the second question: "Does the Howitzer recoil when you shoot?"

I did not know the meaning of the term "recoil," and I told him so. "Sir, I really do not know the term 'recoil.' What does it mean?" He smiled, and without speaking, he touched his left shoulder with his right hand as an explanation. I answered him, "No, sir. It does not recoil, so it is easy to use."

The interviewer smiled, telling me to go to the next station for the oral test. I thought I had passed the first oral test. I went to the second station. There was a Vietnamese second lieutenant whose name was Tam Le; his English was excellent. He spoke Vietnamese with me, telling me to make an English sentence with the word "if" in the conditional sense to refer to something that had not happened in the past. This was not very difficult for me, because I had learned this when I was still a high school student.

The oral test was over. I hoped that I had passed the oral test, but I just waited for God's will. That was the problem. If they needed just a few men, I might fail; if they needed more than five liaison officers to work with the Korean divisions, I still hoped to be selected.

God's Response to My Prayers: "Good News!"

While I still had two months remaining until graduation, my anxiety was reduced a little by the last English test. I prayed that God would help me be selected as a liaison officer. The test was my last hope though. If I were not selected, I would need to ask my platoon leader to make good on his promise to place me in a military academy for safety. I still trusted in the Lord and believed that the English test was a sign of the Lord's miracles to come.

The week before graduation, no one from our class was to leave the academy, so that we might prepare for the ceremony. Not only did we need to practice the ceremonial parade and rehearse, but we needed to ensure our safety and security as well. Relatives were allowed to come visit the Saturday before graduation.

My wife came to visit me. She looked joyful when I told her of my English test results and said I hoped I would not go to the front. Several days later, all of the graduates were gathered, and we stood silently as we waited to receive our military service assignments.

The instructor read my service assignment, which was for Minh Van Lam, the armed forces language school in Saigon. I was surprised and asked myself, *What for?* I didn't understand what my assignment was.

After everyone left, I asked the captain what unit I was to report to. He looked angry and asked me, "Where were you when I made the announcement?"

"I was present but did not understand you."

He reviewed the list of graduates and said again, "Armed forces language school in Saigon."

Still not understanding, I said "What for, captain?"

"To work as an English Instructor. Can you follow what I'm saying, or do I need to say it again?"

I understood, so I said, "No thanks, Captain."

I was surprised by the news and had not expected such happiness and great joy to overwhelm my heart. I went from seeing only the darkness and storms ahead to seeing a destiny full of God's blessings, grace, and mercy. What I didn't quite understand was how this had come to be. How had I gained the position of English instructor when I had applied for a liaison officer, and who could explain this? One of my roommates explained that perhaps the armed forces language school required many instructors, while the liaison officer position required only a few. The additional candidates that applied for the liaison officer position could have been added to the list of instructors. Whatever the reason, I was lucky to have been selected for the armed forces language school.

It was at this time that I finally understood why I had been drafted into the army, why the medical doctor had refused to free me from service, why I had remained in Thu Duc until graduation, and why the liaison officer position was opened and I answered the announcement. This had all come to be so that I could work for the armed forces language school and improve my English so I could serve the Lord in the future. That was God's will, through God's miracles. God answered my prayers to allow me to learn English in a way that I could never have predicted.

The Bible explains God's ways: "For as the heavens are higher than the earth, so are My ways higher than your ways. And My thoughts than your thoughts" (Isaiah 55:9). When things did not happen the way I willed them, I felt uncomfortable, inconvenienced, and angry. I thought the Lord was ignoring my concern and anxiety, thus not answering my prayers. I misunderstood the Lord so much; He was high, and I was so low. I couldn't see the bigger picture.

As I reviewed all of this with those GIs at my father's house, I was amazed at how it had all come to be—everything from the first baccalaureate to the English test that earned me the English instructor position. Only God could do all these things through His compassion and miracles. "How precious is your loving kindness, O God! And the children of men take refuge in the shadow of Your wings" (Psalm 36:7).

General Thieu Van Nguyen, the Republic of Vietnam president, presided over the commencement ceremony for the Twentieth Infantry Officer Class in December 1965. He named the class "Construction," explaining that the graduates of this class would participate in the country's construction for better progress, like that the civilized nations in the world experienced.

As I graduated, I felt joy thinking back to the chaplain's prayers that I not enter into battle. On the contrary, I would work for a language school and study English, an international language I could use in my future professional career and Christian mission. I was so excited for the opportunity to work in the school and learn a new language. My wife attended my ceremony, and she too was joyful that I was going to live in Saigon, safely near her parents' home. Praise the Lord, my God! Hallelujah! Amen!

The Loss of a Motorcycle at Church

After taking ten days off for graduation, I reported to the military school commandant, Lieutenant Colonel Trang Thong Phan, for service. Col. Trang was serious, disciplined, attentive, and hardworking. Eleven graduates of my class at Thu Duc reported to him. He welcomed them and gave some commands: have clean and neat uniforms, and be on time, attentive, hardworking, disciplined, and alert. The new officers took a two-month in-service training class taught by some senior officers. Each new officer was appointed to work for one section. I worked for the training section, under First Lieutenant Dung Van Dang, the chief section. When the training class was over, I was called to present to the commandant.

Here I must relate an unfortunate story that happened to me on the first Lunar New Year's day. My wife's older brother-in-law bought a brand-new motorbike and sold it to me at my request so I could use it to go to work. On the Lunar New Year's Day of 1966, we rode it to Ban Co Church. After the service, we went downstairs and found the motorbike was lost. My father-in-law took me to a former minister to get an old aluminum bicycle that I could use to go to work. My wife's heart was broken, and so was mine. Yet I thought of a kind of a spiritual test after a material blessing.

Back to my meeting after my training class: when I first saluted the commandant, he told me to prepare to move to Da

Nang city, central Vietnam. I asked, "Temporarily or for good, Commandant?"

"For good," he replied.

I asked that he allow me to work for a few months before moving me to Da Nang. He asked why, as this was an urgent order—one that needed to be obeyed. He said, "The recruiting office needs an officer. You can work there, but not here, as your knowledge of English is not good enough to be an instructor. You must leave here."

I said, "Sir, I borrowed a new motorbike, and it was lost on the first New Year's Day. I need to stay here to pay the debt."

He said, "The loss of your motorbike is not involved with the order of your moving. The two things are quite different. But how much is your motorbike?"

"Thirteen thousand piasters."

He asked, "How much was the lock you used for your motorbike?"

"Twenty piasters."

"You used a twenty-piaster lock for a thirteen thousand motorbike? That was the reason for the loss."

Now the commandant and I automatically changed the subject to the loss of the motorbike instead of leaving the school for another unit. He looked at my biography while talking to me. I was silently praying, "Oh, Lord, please tell the commandant to keep me at this school."

He asked, "Were you the elementary school principal?"

"Yes, sir."

"You have two daughters—one born in 1962, and another born in 1964?"

I replied, "Yes, sir."

"My wife is also an elementary school teacher, and my two daughters' birth years are the same as yours. Our school is going to open a Vietnamese class for Korean soldiers. I will keep you at school to run the Vietnamese class for the Korean students—if you think you can do that job?"

I joyfully and immediately answered him, "Yes, sir."

"Leave and tell Phung, your new attendant, to come here. He will replace you at Da Nang."

I went home with joy in my heart and told my wife about the conversation with the commandant. We both were aware of God's involvement. It was one more experience that helped us realize the benefit of these tests. It was like Job's life: After he patiently endured the tests with perseverance, he knew God better than before. The tests were meant to develop his relationship with God. When you experience tests in life, be silent and know that God's children will eventually know God's will. If you try your best to overcome challenges, you will be blessed.

Chapter 11

The Fifth Miracle: Missed Another Bomb Explosion

We had only a brief break for meals, so I stayed at school and took lunch at the restaurant by the joint general staff (JGS) gate. One day after teaching my class, I headed toward the gate for lunch, but I had forgotten my cap. The janitor had locked my classroom, so I stayed around the classroom area asking anyone that was around to let me borrow one during the break. It was ridiculous, but no one would let me borrow one, even just for lunchtime, probably because they saw it as unhygienic.

While I was searching around for a cap, I heard a loud explosion, followed by a second explosion fifteen seconds later. Everyone was frightened, thinking that terrorism had come to our safe haven in South Vietnam. I saw many soldiers run through the gate to the JGS for protection, and they said that two claymore bombs had exploded and killed a lot of soldiers who were eating at the restaurant near the JGS gate. I realized that had I not stopped to search for a cap, I would have been near the gate and likely killed by the explosions. All of these events—me leaving my hat behind, no one lending me one, the janitor locking the classroom—kept me away from danger. Once again I experienced God's miracle, and I think His will was for me to survive so I might serve him in the future.

Chapter 12

What a Strange Disease

I was working as the chief of the Vietnamese section of the school, supervising three new officers and one sergeant. All four of these persons served as elementary school teachers at the Department of Education prior to joining the army and had been selected through a test, just as I was. Every day they recorded their lessons and played those lessons in the classroom so the Korean students could listen.

The length of each class was twelve weeks, and the students were required to take a test in order to graduate. If they learned the Vietnamese language well, they were awarded in the military, and so they worked hard to earn these rewards.

The commencement ceremony for my Vietnamese students was quite important. A Korean lieutenant general attended, and each student received a diploma. These students learned to read and converse in Vietnamese and were recognized for their efforts. Those who attended, including high-ranking officials from Vietnam and Korea, recognized the progress and showed their enthusiasm.

The commandant showed much appreciation toward me as our success added to his good reputation. He loved me and wanted me to move with him if he took a position at a higher level. One day he called me into his office.

"Minh," he said, "I might leave here to take a province chief position, and I want you to follow me. You will receive a promotion in a suitable role. Will you agree to this, as I really need you?"

"Sir, I will do what you want me to do."

"But why do you look so sad these days, Minh? Tell me what has happened, so I can see if might be able to help."

"Sir, my wife has been critically ill."

"What is she sick with?"

"She had an anembryonic pregnancy."

"What's that? I really do not know."

"A kind of pregnancy where an egg is implanted in the uterus but never develops into a embryo or baby. It causes a lot of bleeding."

"Minh, take your wife to one of the better hospitals: Grall, Saint Paul, or the Seventist Hospital."

"The cost is very high, sir, and we are poor."

"I can give you financial support—full coverage for your hospital payment."

"No, Commandant. I don't want to take money from you, as you have your own family to take care of."

"Or you can take your wife to the General Army Medical Hospital. I can call the hospital director, Col. Pham, as he is a close friend of mine and a student here."

"No, Commandant. Because we are living in Ban Co, that hospital is quite far from us. My wife's relatives are visiting her, and that would be too far for them to travel. She is currently hospitalized at the women's hospital, which specializes in pregnancy and delivery."

"I will speak to Lieutenant Vinh then, whose close friend is the medical doctor to Prime Minister Cao Ky."

"Thank you, Commandant."

The conversation was finished, and I left knowing that he really loved me and was trying his best to help during my family's suffering. The following day, I went to Tu Du Women's Hospital after work to visit my wife, but she was not in her bed. Several other patients told me that she had been moved to the best room in the hospital. This surprised me greatly, and so when I found my wife in her large room, I asked her what had happened.

My wife said, "I don't know why so many doctors and nurses came to care for me. They spoke to me as if I were very important and offered to take me downstairs into this private room. I was afraid I'd be lonely, though, so I asked them to bring one other patient into the room with me." Although my wife did not know why this was happening, I knew why. Lieutenant Vinh had spoken with his friend, and the doctor had spoken with the hospital. We believe the hospital staff thought my wife was a relative of the prime minister! We did not pay any expenses for her stay at the hospital. In addition to all of this help, the students in my class raised money and sent it through one of the Korean officers, who then left it on the bed for her.

During my wife's stay in the hospital, I continued to teach Vietnamese classes until the courses were over and I was appointed back to the training section. Around this time, the deputy commandant, Major Quach, told me that the hospital staff said a surgery was not necessary, as the seaweed being used to treat her womb was working. I came to visit my wife, and my mother-in-law told me that my wife was healing well and was okay. She would likely be discharged the day after tomorrow. Praise the Lord for healing my wife.

Chapter 13

The Sixth Miracle: An Overseas Training

The commandant came to me and asked me about my wife's health. I responded that she was doing okay and was gradually healing from her illness. He immediately said, "I have been waiting for her health to improve so that I could let you take an overseas position. Are you now ready transition to this role in the United States?"

I very quickly said, "Yes, sir! It has been my dream to travel to the United States to study and work so that I can improve my language skills."

He said, "You need to review the books for the test, and an American advisory section will be administering the test for overseas training."

I studied English day and night, at school and at home, praying that I could pass this exam and go to the United States to better my English language skills. All five officers from my company took the same test. When the civilian American advisor announced the results, he said the commandant had decided which candidates would leave for the United States, regardless of the exam grade. The commandant called me and let me know that I would be heading to the United States now and the other officers would follow during the next trip.

However, four young officers left with me for the United States on September 13, 1967. At the time of my departure, my oldest daughter was five years old and my youngest was three. I would be overseas for eight months, missing a large chunk of my daughters' lives and my wife. Family members joined the other officers as they prepared for departure. My wife was still recovering from her illness, so she was unfortunately not able to see me off.

We flew Pan Am to San Francisco, with a layover in Guam. We stayed one night in military barracks in San Francisco before flying to San Antonio, Texas. For the next eight months, we called Lackland Air Force Base home. It housed an English-language school belonging to the Defense Language Institute.

After arriving, we were shown to our barracks, which housed two men per room. Orientation followed, and we were introduced to Air Force Major Hoi, a Vietnamese liaison officer and the school commandant. We studied English from Monday through Friday and were given study breaks on Saturdays and Sundays. We went downtown to visit sights such as Flying Ranch, Alamo Village, Fort Alamo, and the San Antonio River. We picnicked and rode horses with cowboys from the area.

I was invited by Chaplain Hien Xuan Pham to sing and share my testimony at a local church. I was the only Christian among the officers that came from Vietnam, and so I was invited to join the church in their Bible study and prayer time at night.

There were several events that occurred through my interaction with this church that I'd like to share:

- While riding in a car with a gentleman named Mr. Nunley (the CMA church treasurer), a rock was thrown into the car by someone's tires while we were driving on the highway. The stone broke the front windshield, and glass injured my face. The other driver stopped to help and took me to a nearby home, where the homeowner allowed us to use the bathroom so that I might clean my face. He called the police, who recommended I visit the army hospital since I was a serviceman. He took me to the hospital, where the medical staff treated me very nicely and the police interviewed me about the event. Praise God that there were no serious injuries and that the situation was handled so nicely! The church members were certainly anxious, since I was a foreigner and in foreign military service.

- An elderly couple at First Baptist Church in Castle Hills sort of adopted me while I was living in the United States. The husband was a veteran US Army major volunteering for the police department, and his wife (originally from Puerto Rico) worked at a dentist's office. They loved me and invited my friends and me over to their home every Sunday. We would attend worship with them and then eat lunch at their home afterward. The husband's mother, Mrs. Albright, often came to San Antonio from Chicago to visit them and she played piano to accompany my singing at church. The churchgoers always welcomed my solos, constantly loving me as I loved them.

- I met another couple that sang every Sunday in worship at a small CMA church in San Antonio. They had two children—a daughter and a son. Their daughter had Down syndrome and died at the age of eight in 1968. I was touched by this family's faithfulness to their service of the Lord during this time tragedy. When I spoke at churches, I often spoke of this couple's experience to show an example of faithfulness and devotion in spite of suffering.

Every time I left the church to return to school, I hated to say good-bye, as they were so dear to me. At school, though, the curriculum was not too challenging. I was able to follow the teacher's explanations. Even though we all felt comfortable with the curriculum, I needed to study whenever I had free time. I ensured I never missed a Sunday at church, so I had to grab free time around that commitment. All the free time in my eight months of study seemed too short to learn all of the English I had hoped to learn.

The Tet of 1968, called Mau Than, was a national tragedy, as fighting broke out in thirty-six major cities in Vietnam. Vietnamese soldiers living outside the country had difficulty studying, as we were constantly waiting to hear news from our families. Several students had been at the school only a few days before they heard of a death in the family and had to return to Vietnam to bury their relatives. Those that remained at the school often missed meals to watch special reports on the Vietnam War. No one felt peace waiting for news from his or her family. Everything seemed to be clouded in sadness as we all waited for the time to go by so we could go home. In April of 1968, the four other officers and I were able to return home. We had ten days off after we presented to the commandant for service in Vietnam.

Chapter 14

The Seventh Miracle: A Miraculous Discharge

After presenting ourselves for service, we were each appointed to the sections we had left before going to the United States. I worked in the training position until the commandant received an order from the joint general staff to transfer from the Armed Forces Language School to the Fifth Office of the Joint General Staff. Major Huynh, who was the former administrative officer to the school, returned to be the commandant and asked me to leave the training section to be the company leader for the interpreters.

In 1969, the National Defense Department and the National Education Department collectively agreed to release twelve thousand elementary, high school, and college teachers from their military service. They were to be appointed back to their former civilian positions, as the schools needed the educators. Unfortunately this excluded military schools, such as Da Lat National Military Academy, the Youth Military School, and the Armed Forces Language School, which meant I was not allowed to return to my elementary school because of the army's need. The miracle in this was that it allowed me to strengthen my faith in God.

God's Miracles

One evening I went to a large church on Tran Hung Dao Street in Saigon to hear an evangelist preach. I met my wife's older brother in the church's front yard, and he asked me why I hadn't come home to Soc Trang when the other teachers returned to their schools. I said, "My unit is a military language school, and the agreement does not allow for my discharge."

He said, "The church pastor is old and weak; he is unable to run the church smoothly and needs you to help contribute to its growth."

I did not promise anything to him, as I believed I was committed to the military and law would not allow me to leave to help. However, his words made me think a great deal of the church in Soc Trang, where I had accepted the Lord, received baptism, experienced spiritual growth, wed, and dedicated our children. I wanted to do something for the church.

That night I prayed to the Lord that He might bring me back to Soc Trang to serve Him. I decided to sign a form to request a special assignment at the administration section. After I while, I forgot about my request and continued to work peacefully at the military language school.

About a month later, Major Gam van Nguyen of the administration office met me at school and shouted loudly, "Lieutenant Minh, you made the commandant instruct me to discharge you."

I said, "I really do not know what you mean, Major!"

"The Department of Defense is allowing you to go back to teach at your former school. If you want to know the truth about it, go to Lieutenant Bang's office."

"Thank you, Major" I said.

I went to the administration section to see Lieutenant Bang, the section chief. He showed me the special assignment orders that the general had signed, permitting me to return to teaching at my former school.

I need to interrupt the story to stress how much of a miracle this actually was in my life. Only a miracle could explain how I received a special assignment letting me return to civilian life when the agreement between the two national departments did not allow this to be.

I needed to speak to the commandant to really understand what had happened. When I went into his office, it appeared he was very angry to see me. He said, "Sit down. I have spent an entire day investigating how your special assignment was approved."

He told me of an investigation where he had met two colonels of the joint general staff to ask the captain to explain the special order approval. They had asked the captain, "Why did Lieutenant Minh Van Lam receive the order of special assignment after he has been in the army only five years? Another captain has been in for seven years and is also a former teacher; why was he not given a special order?" The captain searched for the file on the other teacher but was unable to locate it.

My commandant said, "Lieutenant Minh Van Lam has trained in the United States for eight months; he should not be allowed to leave the army without serving two more years." The captain searched for my documentation regarding the overseas training but was again unable to find the documentation. Since there was no documentation on our cases, the colonels offered a few suggestions. They suggested that the captain send a request for an important mission that I needed to serve on. They said they would send the request to the Department of Defense and that would keep me in the army. In one day, this problem could be solved.

The commandant told me that he said he would think on the suggestion and respond to them within the day. But he decided that if I were forced to stay, I would not have the spirit to serve here any longer. In his opinion, it was best just to let me leave. He told me to remember that once I left, I could never return to the language school. But if I decided to stay and work here, he would promote me to captain and allow me to train in the United States one more time. He told me to think about it and get back to him.

Although there were benefits to staying, there was no question. I would leave the language school to teach in the civilian school again and serve the Lord. I didn't give a response immediately and was assigned to make a table of organization and equipment (TOE) so the commandant could be promoted to full colonel. Since I had not yet given a response to the commandant, he believed I had refused his suggestion and was quite upset with me. I received an order to report to his office so I could prepare to leave military service. I said good-bye to everyone I had met and come to care for at the language school. Some of them said I would regret my decision, as I would not be promoted and would eventually be called back to fight. Those threats did not change my mind, as I had decided that serving the Lord was my first priority. I would gladly accept any suffering just to serve Him.

When I reported to the personnel office at the National Department of Education, a man asked me how I could possibly be discharged for civilian life, since my military unit was at the Armed Forces Language School. I said, "I really don't know; everyone seems surprised, but I am just following orders." He confirmed that I would be appointed back to Ba Xuyen, and I joyfully said good-bye to everyone in the office. I was leaving my military service behind, along with all of the discipline, absolute obedience, strictness, clean and neat uniforms, punctuality, and punishment. Even though I was happy to be leaving, I was glad about the English knowledge I had obtained, the military experiences I had received, and the US training I had taken part in.

In addition, during my military time, I was awarded a continuing education diploma from the National Department of Education in Saigon, an English-language teacher diploma from the English language school associated with the Defense Language Institute in the United States, and credits from the overseas training in the United States. I was proud of my five years of military service and thankful for the material and spiritual compensation. I believed the Lord answered my prayers to learn the English language and placed me into military service at the Armed Forces Language School for those prayers to be answered. I praise the Lord for His will, grace, and miracles in my life. I gave thanks for His power and blessings, and I felt very confident coming back to serve in my former province.

Most soldiers in military service would probably have taken the commandant's suggestion and stayed in the army to be promoted and get praise and honor. I, however, ignored that suggestion for several reasons.

1. I did not want to displease my Lord, who heard my prayer and performed a miracle in discharging me from the army. I think the Lord would be angry with me if I asked for something and then refused it.
2. I had loved my former occupation since I was a child. My joy was in teaching the kids.
3. I loved my church in Soc Trang and wanted to see it improved; therefore, I needed to help the pastor.
4. The Lord miraculously allowed the two national departments to discharge me because of His future plans for my life. I'll discuss this more later, but if I had stayed and been promoted to captain, I would have been a prisoner of war for seven years in North Vietnam, rather than the three years I spent in a local area.

5. My wife would not have given birth to more children if I had stayed in the army.
6. I would not have been promoted to teach high school if I had stayed in the army.
7. I would not have had the financial support to escape Vietnam by boat if I had not been in Soc Trang through 1975.

Time has flown by, and as I write this, it has been nearly forty-five years since this decision was made in 1970. I am joyful that I made this decision, guided by the Holy Spirit, so that I might have obtained such tremendous results. The Lord's plan has been very good for my whole family and me. Hallelujah! Amen. Praise the Lord. I had left the military service and was ready to begin the chapter of my life in which I would serve the Lord Jesus!

Section IV

God's Miracles for My Christian Life

Chapter 15
Two More Children

God Gave Us Two More Children

As we left Saigon for Soc Trang in July of 1970, we said goodbye to my in-laws. My older brother Kiet Van Lam drove us to the western bus station in his Daihatsu. Von also came with us to Soc Trang; he was an employee of my in-laws but decided to return to his hometown. My wife's mother cried so much, and my brother spent a lot of time comforting her. She was surprised and touched that we left her all of the money we had made while living with her but had nothing to take with us as we left for Soc Trang. I believed that we had honored my parents during our stay with them in Soc Trang and that it was only right for us to honor my wife's parents while we stayed with them. We were still young enough to earn more funds, and the Lord would bless us in the future for honoring our parents.

We stayed in my parents' house for three days, and I said to my father, "Dad, I prayed to the Lord that if I were allowed to return to my former career, then I would live near the church to serve the Lord. We have stayed here for three days, but now we must leave for the church." I had previously sent an application to Pastor Tam so that I might stay near the church and serve by cleaning the church, providing security, or growing trees. Pastor Tam gave the application to Rev. Nguyen, who was in charge of all Vietnamese Evangelical Churches in the western region. After receiving the application, he agreed to accept it, as he knew that I was spiritual and helpful.

My older brother Hoi Van Lam's family came with us to live near the church. We asked a local home builder to build us a house with a roof made of coconut leaves and walls made of thin roofing iron. My brother's family lived in the upper level, and my family resided in the lower level of the home. We shared one of our walls with the church building, which provides an idea of how close we were able to reside to the church. Our lodging was several meters from the parsonage, where the pastor resided.

My brother was elected by the congregation to serve as a committee deacon before we arrived at Soc Trang. Though I was not elected, the congregation loved me because I had been active before my military service. The church ran an elementary school consisting of three classes from kindergarten through second grade. The parsonage was used as the school location, but the school board planned to build a two-story concrete building beside the parsonage. I helped the school board through my knowledge of English by talking to the US Air Force officers at the airport, police advisors, and Seabee engineer soldiers, and by mailing letters to American Christians in the United States that I had met when studying overseas. The construction of the school was soon completed. There were six classrooms on each floor, housing classes from kindergarten through sixth grade. Mrs. Hien served as principal, and I was elected board secretary. I also translated for American preachers who visited our church.

Almost every evening, I stepped into the parsonage to chat with the pastor. One night he said, "You have just the two daughters, don't you?"

"Yes, sir. I'd like to have a son, but it is impossible for my wife."

He said, "Let's pray and ask the Lord to give you a son. It is impossible for man, but not for God." The pastor immediately bowed his head and prayed, "Oh, dear Lord, we ask you to give Mr. Minh one son. He promises to offer that son for the Lord to use. In the name of the Lord Jesus Christ, I pray. Amen!"

One month later, my wife was not feeling very well. She went to the doctor and came home to tell me that she was pregnant. I was surprised and said, "This happened so quickly; how did this happen?" I then said, "The pastor recently prayed with me at his parsonage for this, and now you are pregnant."

My wife said, "The Lord heard his prayers and immediately answered them. Let him know about my pregnancy, and remember to thank him."

She said, "He asked the Lord to give us a son. If a son is born, we'll offer him to the Lord to use for His service."

There was an old man named Mr. Tran who had severe stomach cancer. Two days before his death, he was brought home from the hospital. Several church members surrounded him to pray. Looking at everyone, he said, "Don't pray for me to live. I have seen heaven already, which means I am going there to see the Lord. Who here needs something? Tell me, and I will tell the Lord when I see him."

I said to him, "Uncle Nine, I ask you to tell the Lord that I am asking for a son, since I only have daughters." He said, "Don't worry; I'll tell the Lord for you."

My wife gave birth to a son on May 20, 1971, at Khanh Hung Hospital. I rode around the city on my Honda motorbike, telling all my relatives that a son had just been born to us. It was God's miracle to my wife, who was told during her embryonic treatment that she would never have a successful pregnancy. Because the pastor had said, "It is impossible for man, but not for the Lord!" I named him Ai Duy Lam. "*Ai*" means "love," "*Duy*" means "just," and Lam is our family name. "*Duy Ai*" means "just the love," based on "God is love" (1 John 4:8) and "but the greatest of these is love" (1 Corinthians 13:13b). This miracle was God's love.

In 1972, we built a house in the handicapped veteran village on Phu Loi Road of Khanh Hung Village in the Soc Trang province. We shared two of our walls with the neighboring houses.

Two years after Ai's birth, another daughter was born into our family on May 11, 1973. We named her Linh Thuy Lam. "*Linh*" means "soul or spirit," and "*Thuy*" means "gentle." Together her name means "gentle soul or spirit." We chose this name from the Lord Jesus Christ's statements "For what will it profit a man if he gains the whole world and forfeits his soul? Or what will a man give in exchange for his soul?" (Matthew 16:26) and "Do not fear those who kill the body but are unable to kill the soul; but rather fear Him who is able to destroy both soul and body in hell" (Matthew 10:28).

My wife gave birth to two children in two years. The Lord showed his power and his miracles to us by giving children to a woman who doctors said could never give birth.

A High School Teacher

Prior to joining the army, I was teaching at the elementary school level. When I presented myself to the elementary school superintendent for service, he appointed me to teach English at a middle school in Soc Trang. Perhaps he was told about my time in the Armed Forces Language School and my overseas English training. I was also given the opportunity to teach English at a private high school where one of my former teachers was now principal. In order to teach middle school, I needed to take an examination organized by the National Department of Education. I passed the examination, but the public and private high schools asked me to teach the high school senior grade. I began teaching at Tran Van Private High School. It had six classrooms, two for each grade from tenth through twelfth. I was in charge of all those taking English language courses as either their first or second foreign language. Students in the private and public high schools loved me. Some of them were so interested in learning English that they switched it from their second language to their first.

The house we built was constructed using not only our money but also my father's money. Our house was four meters wide, eighteen meters long, and had a rainwater cistern inside for drinking and cooking. This was the first house our family lived in that was our own since 1973, when our first daughter was born. We used the home in the evening and during the summer for additional English classes. The students made the blackboard and student table and then delivered the items to my house as a gift for me to use while teaching at home.

I was also teaching English at several high schools around the city and studying to obtain a bachelor of arts at the Faculty of Letters in Saigon. I passed the first-year examination in 1974 and prepared for the second-year examination in 1975. Can you imagine the schedule I had? I taught twelve hours a day, from 7:00 a.m. to noon, from 1:00 p.m. to 6:00 p.m., and from 7:00 p.m. to 9:00 p.m., six days a week. All of the hard work and continuous studying made me quite skinny! In addition, while I was doing this, I was serving as the Samuel Elementary School Board secretary, sending English correspondence to American benefactors in the United States for financial support. Lastly, I was taking Bible lessons from the Gospel Theological Institute. Only through God's miracles was I able to do these important jobs for my church. My five years of military service in Saigon helped prepare me to serve the Lord at church, teach English, and study for my future professional career and theological teaching on missions in Soc Trang, Thailand refugee camps, the United States, and in the word.

Usually during God's tests during biblical times, while tragedy and suffering were present, advantages and benefits also came to the Lord's children if they applied the biblical lessons of God's favored people to their own lives. Joseph, for example, was sold by his brothers to be a slave; and Job, who was damaged by Satan and blamed by his friends for his sufferings, also received great blessings. Joseph answered the Egyptian king, "It is not in me; God will give Pharaoh a favorable answer" (Genesis 41:16). And Job confessed to God, "Therefore I have declared that which I did not understand, things too wonderful for me, which I did not know" (Job 4:3b).

It's so strange and wonderful that a poor and unhealthy boy, then an elementary school teacher with poor English language skills living in a rural village, was reluctantly drafted into the army and trained to fight but was miraculously transformed into a high school English teacher. All of this happened as a result of my prayers based on the story of the languages created during the construction of the Tower of Babel. (See Genesis 11:1–9.) From these prayers stemmed nearly fifteen years of teaching in Vietnam. I served as an elementary school teacher from 1959–1965, an English instructor to soldiers at the Armed Forces Language School from 1966–1970, and a high school English teacher from 1970–1975.

The fall of Saigon in 1975 was a turning point in the war, and these events contributed to a turning point in my own life from 1995 through 2009, during which time I taught the Bible at a Bible college in the United States. Praise the Lord for the teaching career He gave me after my graduation from the National Pedagogy School.

Chapter 16
A Helpful Presentation

I had been teaching high school for five years when the Communist forces attacked and seized South Vietnam. I had forgotten that I was still in the military, as I had traded my uniform, insignia, and guns for the classroom. It was for this reason that I neglected to present myself when government agencies announced that all South Vietnamese soldiers and civil servants needed to report for duty; I didn't realize I needed to. On June 6, 1975, I drove my motorbike to My Xuyen Elementary School to report to them. I remained there overnight with eleven other teachers who had previously served as army officers. That night a man in civilian clothing came to our room and told us that we were secret agents that told police officers to arrest countrymen who admitted to loving Vietnam and serving as patriots. One of my female students rode by bicycle to my home and told my wife that I had been caught as a prisoner of war.

I thought he must have misunderstood us, thinking that we had returned to civilian life to do such things. I had hope that the new government would listen to our explanation and know the truth. The next morning, my wife came by bicycle to bring me money, a pocket-size New Testament Bible, a toothbrush, and toothpaste. I tried to console her by ensuring her God would protect me. After my wife left, the other teachers and I were guided to the boat at the river to be moved to another place.

We came to a little village near a big river and stayed at an elementary school for twenty-four days. Each of us was asked to report on what we had done during our military service; I was the last to be interviewed. We were then transported back to Soc Trang, where we stayed for a month and half in the jail of the former government. Can you imagine someone going two and half months without having a bowel movement and still living? That was the position I was in. I believe I survived because of God's love and miracles. I moved to eight different camps in the rural countryside, doing manual labor.

My wife visited me once a month to give me some food and money and tell me about the children, our parents, and the happenings at home. One month she wasn't able to come, though, as she was in the hospital with our youngest child, who had hemorrhagic fever. I was imprisoned, my wife had no employment, my children were little, and we had no money to buy medications or pay the doctors; we were broken. We prayed to the Lord for healing and relied on God for a miracle. Fortunately, the Lord heard our prayers and our child recovered; many other children died from the epidemic.

One day there was commotion at a rice field camp. The prisoners were ordered to gather for a control and status check to ensure everyone was accounted for. Three prisoners did not report. Later that evening, when they returned, the chief asked them, "Where did you go today, as I observed your absence during this morning's check-in?" They told him that they had gone to find food, such as fish, mice, or fruit. He said, "You said you had diarrhea. How could you go find food when you were sick?"

They said, "We tried to."

"No, you lie. I accuse you of contacting a rebellious force to attack our camp. How do you answer me?"

They kept silent. Fifty prisoners in the camp were silent too. Then the camp chief asked, "Do any of you have any information regarding these men's absence today?" Nobody wanted to be involved, as it was very dangerous to speak up. He then asked the group leaders if they knew, and they all remained silent as well.

I raised my hand and said, "I have an idea, sir. I don't really know where these men went today, but I ask that you forgive them. If they had contacted the rebel forces, they would not have returned tonight. They were trying to increase their labor so that they may earn credits and be released sooner, according to camp rules. They declared that they were sick so they could spend their time searching for food. Surely if they do this again, they will be seriously punished."

He said, "Yes, I forgive them. But remember: they will be put in a cell if they violate the camp law again. Dismissed!"

That night someone told me that the prisoner leader had intended to let the camp chief punish one of the prisoners that he hated, but I had helped them. Someone told me to be wary of the prisoner leader, as I may have upset him by speaking out. One week later, my name was on the list of unhealthy prisoners who had to stay in the central city prison. The prisoner leader did not want me to stay at the rice field camp anymore. The prison in central Soc Trang was not as comfortable as the one in the rice field camp. I was kept in a restricted facility with no freedom. At the prison, I was the group leader and supervised several prisoners while we made a fish pond and an orchard for the chief jailor. He noticed the good work I was doing and recommended me for release from the reeducation camp.

I was officially released on September 15, 1977, which is also my birthday. I suddenly was able to go home and see my parents.

Through God's miracles, I was set free from imprisonment. If I had never spoken up that night in the rice field camp, I would likely still be there. Praise the Lord for all of the events that got me to where I am. I praise Him for the twenty-seven month reeducation in Soc Trang, for my children being healed from their epidemic, and for finally being released from prison. Little did I know that all of these things would bring me to His miracle of a boat rescue in the future!

Chapter 17

The Eighth Miracle: My Canoe Was Not Caught

My wife's brother organized an attempt for us to flee Vietnam by crossing the Pacific Ocean in a wooden boat. He took advantage of the lunar year of 1979, while everyone was home celebrating with family and enjoying the New Year, as this would mean less control and follow-up by the local government officials. That night he let several small groups go before him and wait in bushes near the coastal area so that the main boat under his command could come pick up each group, in order that they might escape the coastal guards.

His boat was drifting through the water, trying to find us in the smaller boats that were hiding in the bushes. Unfortunately he couldn't find anyone, and as he was looking, the coast guard police seized his boat. We were nearby in the bushes and heard many gunshots and believed that he had been caught. We were anxious all night.

If his boat had found our small group and picked us up, we would have been with him and arrested for many years, which is what happened to him. We believe the Lord protected us by hiding us from both his boat and the coast guard. The next day, we were able to return to the village we had departed from. We prayed for him and his family, thankful that we were able to go home through God's protection.

Chapter 18
The Visions for the Flight

My Visions

Return with me for a moment to my imprisonment in the rice field camp. After having our early morning meal, I followed the camp leader (who was also a prisoner) to the rice field to dig in the ground. I worked very hard but felt comfortable for some reason. My wife could visit me anytime, I could swim in the river to bathe, I could catch fish for meals, and I had fresh air for breathing.

After work and dinner one evening, I went to bed early in preparation for the next day's hard work. I slept well this night and dreamed that I took a trip to a Western country where I met people that looked like Europeans and Americans. I spoke to them in the dream, and they said I was to stay with them and work and preach. After waking, I had happy thoughts of the dream while I was eating my meal. I thought the dream was quite strange, though, as I was currently imprisoned and also because I was not yet a preacher.

That was the first time I had a vision that I would cross the ocean. The second vision would come later, after I was released from prison. Before I had that vision, I began organizing our trip to flee Vietnam. We had to leave the home we built because an official from the new government did not believe that a man from the reeducation camps had the right to live in the big city. So we moved to a small village named Thanh Quoi—Tra Cuon in Khmer—which was about twenty-four kilometers from Soc Trang. We lived next to my older sister's house and worked like peasants in 1977. We were very broken. I was in a probationary period after my release from the reeducation camps. Our income was not enough for our six-person family, so my sixteen-year-old daughter had to work as a maid for her aunt in Saigon. The village officials told us that they had received orders from the government to kill all former prisoners of war in the event that China invaded. The thread of poverty, imprisonment, and death were reasons for us to flee our dear country. We just didn't know how we would organize a trip when we were too poor to travel. We had nothing but prayers to bring to God. Jeremiah 33:3 says, "Call to Me and I will answer you, and I will tell you great and mighty things, which you do not know." We knew this verse by heart and read it at every prayer meeting after evening meal.

Our prayer was answered through two female students who offered a little money, as they also wanted to participate in the trip. The next day, I went to church to speak to some Christians about crossing the ocean. I spoke to several others about money, and everyone I spoke with agreed to join us. I finally got enough money to buy a little old wooden boat with an old engine. The boat was repaired so that it could handle crossing the ocean. I said that if we arrived safely on the mainland, I would serve the Lord in ministry. I prayed specifically for three things:

1. No one would get lost going from the small canoes to the main boat during the night.

2. We would have enough protection from the heavy rain and the engine sound reduction would be enough to keep us from being heard.
3. We would be rescued by an American ship.

My father died from diabetes in September 1980, twenty days before our trip. I slept in his bed, where he had lain during several years of sickness. One night close to the departure day, I prayed before bed, "Oh dear heavenly Father, we are about to flee from Vietnam, and we ask you to give us a sign as to whether we can escape or not. In the name of the Lord Jesus Christ, I pray. Amen."

That night I had a dream, which I believe was a vision encouraging me to boldly cross the Pacific Ocean. In the vision I saw that my boat lost its way and we didn't know where to go. I prayed. The Lord appeared standing on the water, wearing a long white robe, with long hair, pointing toward the left. He said, "Go there!" and then disappeared. Our boat continued on until we arrived at the large white ship, which immediately picked us up and took us safely to the mainland. After I woke, I told my mother that our trip would be successful. My mother asked me how I knew, and I explained my vision. Since that dream, I was very interested in the details of the boat.

We showed the six canoe leaders the main boat the night before our departure so they would be able to recognize it. The canoes would be coming from various rivers to meet the main boat on the large river. The canoe leaders would need to recognize the boat and arrive on time, as anyone late would be abandoned. My old wooden boat was about thirty feet long and ten feet wide, and it would hold forty-seven refugees: twenty-four men, thirteen women, and ten children. The youngest was a twenty-month-old little girl. The main boat departed the riverbank near the residential area of Dai Ngai market on October 3, 1980, at

7:00 p.m. There wasn't a cloud in the sky as we pulled out, but as we moved down the small river, a heavy rain poured for several hours, lasting until we could see the ocean.

When our boat arrived near the beach, we heard gunshots, but I said to the group, "Continue on. Don't fear, and don't stop." It took us five hours to move safely from the small river into the Pacific Ocean. When we were finally at the ocean, the rain stopped and let us run smoothly. I raised my hands and prayed, "Oh, dear Lord, thank you so much for gathering the six canoes with no one left behind. Thank you for bringing us safely. Now, as we leave Vietnam territory, we are in your hands. Please take us safely to an American ship to be rescued."

We spent all night struggling with big waves while several large ships passed by us. Even though we burned cloth as our SOS sign, they did not rescue us. The next day, our navigator, looking quite tired, said to me, "I don't know which direction Malaysia is." I remembered my dream and prayed. I asked my former high school student, Nga, if she knew the direction of Malaysia, as she was a second-year college student at the School of Pedagogy in Can Tho, studying geography. She gave me the coordinates that she remembered from school, and I gave those to the navigator. As we were traveling toward those coordinates, a storm came in. I saw a blue line appear from west to east in front of us at the horizon and asked the navigator what that was, wondering if it might be the mainland. He said, "No, it's a big wave."

"How can we escape it?" I asked.

"Impossible," he said.

The Ship First Mate's Vision of My Boat

I asked the Lord to still the storm and waves. The storm caused some damage to the boat, and my wife and I went into the hold to bail out water that was coming in. As we were working, someone shouted, "A big ship is coming toward us!"

My wife said, "Continue praying, as many ships have come and left us."

I changed my prayer: "Oh dear Lord. Please command the ship's captain to stop and rescue us. Our boat is going to sink."

For a while I heard people saying, "The ship has completely stopped and is waiting for us to come."

Why did the ship completely stop? I thought. *To pick us up?* We did not know, but unbeknownst to us, the first mate had a vision that he later told to us in Long Beach, California. Following is the story of that vision.

***

Mr. Blaine Buckley, the former first mate of the ship *Leslie Lykes*, said to us, "I had a dream the night before we saw your boat on the surface of the Pacific Ocean. In the dream, I saw a little wooden boat full of men, women, and children. When they saw our ship coming, the people raised their hands as an SOS sign. We heard their cries echoing toward us; they were yelling 'Help!' as they wept and shouted. The cries in the dream woke me, as the sun had not yet risen. I rose and immediately took my binoculars to scan the ocean from east to west and south to north. The captain asked me why I was watching the ocean so carefully, and I told him I had seen a refugee boat in my dream last night. I don't know if the captain believed me, but I scanned the ocean until I recognized your boat. When I saw a faint image of a boat, I was sure my dream was coming true. I told the captain to stop the ship. He asked why, and I said, 'To rescue the refugees in that boat coming toward us.' The captain said, 'We cannot do that, as our ship is not responsible for such a mission. I don't want to get in trouble if the Thailand government does not agree to accept them.'

The captain and I argued about the rescue, and he finally accepted my compromise. He stopped our boat to assess the approaching boat and wait."

***

When I heard the people on my boat say the ship had stopped, I told the navigator to go straight to the ship. He hesitated, saying, "If it is Russian, how can we cope with such a problem?"

I said, "I am responsible for that." I didn't want to tell him that our boat was going to sink soon and that our first priority was a rescue; otherwise, everyone would die. The type of ship we were rescued by was no longer our biggest problem.

Chapter 19

The Ninth Miracle: Boat Rescue

As we approached the big ship, I shouted so everyone could hear. "Ladies and gentlemen, we are Vietnamese refugees that have just come from Vietnam. Our boat is sinking; please rescue us!"

Someone from the boat said, "Our ship transports wheat and passengers to Thailand; we are not responsible for refugees."

I was so happy to hear an American accent, so I tried again. "Ladies and gentlemen, please rescue us! The women and children are seasick, and we will die if you don't help. I pray to the Lord Jesus Christ to bless you, your ship, your family, and your country. Please help, as we really need your help!"

I prayed for them because I hoped that someone hearing us was a Christian who would ask the captain to rescue us. They lowered a ladder and said that I could embark, but no one else could come aboard yet. When I arrived at the top, a man asked if we were Chinese, and I told him that we were not Chinese but were Vietnamese refugees. He began speaking to the men around him and commented on how well I spoke English. He took me to the captain, who asked, "Where are you going?"

"We are seeking political protection, sir."

He said, "This is a merchant vessel, and we can't be responsible for refugees. If the Thai government does not accept you, I don't know where we could take you."

I said, "You can drop us on any island, as our boat is broken and will sink at any time."

"No, we cannot do that, but we can give you what you need to go on your own way."

The first mate, Mr. Blaine Buckley, spoke up strongly, saying, "If you let these people go their own way, you are sentencing them to a burial at sea."

The captain said, "I will make a call." He called someone, though I do not know whom. I assume he called the US Embassy to approve the rescue. Everyone except the first mate left the area. I thanked him for interfering on our behalf, which had prompted the captain to call for help. He answered me, "Don't worry; I will try my best to help you. I am a Christian like you."

The captain returned after about fifteen minutes and said they would accept a rescue. I wanted to cry out in extreme joy, and I felt my eyes fill with tears. My heart beat very fast as I experienced God's miracle in response to my prayer. My vision came true of God's presence on the largest ocean in the world, to save poor Vietnamese lives and souls.

The two daughters of Dr. Minh Van Lam were praying for the boat rescue at sea on October 5, 1980.

The first mate took me to a place where I could see the people on our little boat. They were frightened and calling for help, safety, and protection. I said to them, "Do not cry. We are going to be rescued. Good news!"

I heard several Christians on the boat shout, "Hallelujah! Praise the Lord!" Other passengers pulled out handkerchiefs to dry their tears.

I said, "Crawl to the hold of the boat and search for anyone still there. Let the children go first, then the women, the sick, and lastly the remaining men. Go in that order, and do not jostle each other!"

The seamen used a sling to beautifully and successfully bring all of the people onto the ship in just a few minutes. Once everyone was standing on the ship, seamen counted everyone for control purposes and announced, "Forty-seven people, including ten children, thirteen women, and twenty-four men." They smiled happily at us and left to continue their work.

My wife and I were told to see a seaman so that the old wooden boat could be cut loose. We loved the boat, as it had taken us from Vietnam safely. We didn't want to see if off, but we knew we could not keep it with us forever.

We were allowed to stay at the stern of the ship during the voyage to Thailand. We were given water, a meal to eat, clothes donated by other passengers, and a little money to spend in the refugee camp (also donated by passengers).

Our Meeting with Mr. Blaine Buckley and His Wife, D. Anne

I'll continue with the rest of the story in a moment. It's important to first share a meeting we had later with Mr. Blaine Buckley in Hawthorne, Los Angeles, California, in January 1981, after first arriving in the United States. After we arrived in Hawthorn City on January 16, 1981, I called Mr. Buckley at the home phone number he had given me during our stay with him and his wife in Thailand. His wife picked up the phone, we spoke, and they made plans to come see us. We were so joyful that we could see our benefactor, Mr. Buckley, who had insisted on our rescue. It was on this day that he shared the reason why he had wanted to pick us up that day on the ocean—the story of his vision. After hearing his story, I believed the Lord was most certainly involved on the Pacific Ocean. The Lord had heard my prayers and had not only given me a dream of our crossing but had also given Mr. Blaine Buckley a dream that prompted him to patiently but persistently ask the captain to rescue us. It verified the Lord's omniscience, omnipresence, and omnipotence while pushing us to continue trusting in the Lord and doing His work.

I was like a younger adopted brother to the Buckleys. One night Mr. Buckley called to let me know that he was in Kansas at his farm and would like to come visit me in Fort Smith, Arkansas. We loved each other greatly. I told him that when they became too old to care for themselves, I would assign one of my children to take care of them. He smiled happily but said, "It's not necessary; our children will care for us, but thank you for your concern." We made those kinds of gestures to one another.

We moved to Virginia in 1987 and were shocked to hear the sad news of Blaine's sudden passing during a stomach surgery at the Guam Military Hospital. His water burial was held in Guam, but a memorial service was being held at First United Methodist Church in Long Beach, California, afterward. My wife and two youngest children, Ai and Linh, went with me to attend the service. I read my testimony of the boat rescue, and their hearts were touched and they wept.

After his death, I contacted his wife as often as I could and visited with my family. In September 2012, on the occasion of Ai's wedding, I went to visit her. Her son Matthew met me at the door and told me that she had gone to be with the Lord in May of 2008. I was so sorrowful that I cried, despite her having passed after living a long life. He son handed me her Bible and said that she had asked the children to give the Bible to me upon her passing so that I could use it for my own reading and studying.

I strongly believe that my brother Blaine and my sister D. Anne were face-to-face with their Lord Jesus Christ right after their passing. They had such strong faith in Him, and they did what He instructed during the boat rescue. He was not afraid of being fired; rather he remained persistent. He was later fired when they returned to the United States, in part because of the argument with the captain. He was not unhappy, and I comforted him with words that his actions in rescuing the refugees would be rewarded in heaven when he was taken to heaven after his physical death.

Later D. Anne received a letter of appreciation that I sent regarding Blaine and all of his good deeds during our stay on the ship. One day in particular, he saw me and gave me a yellow envelope with money in it. He said, "Be careful when you arrive in Thailand; keep the money safe from thieves so you and your family may use it." D. Anne replied to me and asked if we needed anything more. I wrote her and let her know that the money had been shared among others who were in need as well. She then sent three hundred US dollars to missionary Rev. D. K. and asked him to exchange it to Thai baht for me. When we left Vietnam, we did not bring any money for our family to use, so we were so thankful for the gift that D. Anne and Blaine gave us. It provided our family and some other people enough funds for our stay in the refugee camp. Their generosity reminded me of the ram Abraham offered to God at the place he named "the Lord Will Provide" (Genesis 22:13–14), as well as the letter Paul wrote to the Philippian church for financial support: "after I left Macedonia, no church shared with me in the matter of giving and receiving but you alone; for even in Thessalonica you sent a gift more than once for my needs" (Philippians 4:15–16).

The Lord provided me with gifts from my brother and sister in Christ—very precious and helpful gifts. I would like to repeat what the apostle Paul wrote to the Corinthian church when he emphasized the church in Macedonia's efforts to help poor Christians in Jerusalem during famine and starvation: "For I testify that according to their ability, and beyond their ability, they gave of their own accord, begging us with much urging for the favor of participation in the support of the saints" (2 Corinthians 8:3–4). Paul gave the Macedonian church credit, saying, "Now He who supplies seed to the sower and bread for food will supply and multiply your seed for sowing and increase the harvest of your righteousness; you will be enriched in everything for all liberality, which through us is producing thanksgiving to God" (2 Corinthians 9:10–12). My dear brother and sister in Christ, what you did for me and forty-six other Vietnamese refugees was undoubtedly rewarded with precious heavenly compensations when you went to see our Lord.

A sailor from the *Leslie Lykes* who lived in Seattle, Washington, took several pictures of our boat rescue and sent thirty-two pictures to me. Since we moved many times, I lost pictures over the years, but many copies still remain, and I have included them in this book. He wrote an article about the rescue and published by the local newspaper in Seattle, Washington. Thankfully Blaine was able to give me a copy of the newspaper so that I could include pieces of that in the book as well.

My Prayers after the Boat Rescue

While everyone was asleep at the stern, I called my wife to kneel down and pray with me. "My dear Lord Jesus Christ, I thought we, like Lazarus, had just risen from the grave on the Pacific Ocean. From now on, I, Minh Van Lam, am now your servant and will serve you until my death. Please take us to the United States at your will. I pray in the name of the Lord Jesus Christ. Amen!" My eyes overflowed with tears that rolled down my cheeks.

The seamen called me to stand and see some lights that were ahead on the ocean. They said it was a gathering of Thai pirates who would have raped, robbed, and murdered the people on our boat. They said we were fortunate, as one more day on the ocean and we would have met those pirates, and they would have brought suffering and tragedy.

Hearing those words, I felt very bad for people on boats that were not rescued. I prayed as I looked out at the waves rolling in front of me, "Oh my dear Lord, Jesus Christ, when I accepted you as my personal Savior, I knew you were powerful because you are God, the Creator. You made the first man, Adam, by dust; you gave us marriage. You made the flood to punish the wicked sinners who did not put trust in you. You created the languages of the world. You founded the Israelites. The Lord Jesus came from heaven to earth to die on the cross for all of mankind. You have mercy, grace, and compassion for the poor, the widows, and the orphans.

"I myself have experienced your love and compassion as you have heard my prayers. I was born into a poor family and was physically unhealthy. I prayed to you, asking for good health so that I could live until I was eighteen, that I might be able to provide my parents with money. I asked to be selected by the vocational schools, and both the commerce and pedagogy schools selected me. I became an elementary school principal. I married according to your will, and in 1965 I was drafted into the army. You took me into the Infantry Military Academy for training and allowed me to work in the Armed Forces Language School in Saigon. I was poor, but you favored me and brought me to the United States to study English. Thanks to the overseas training, I became a high school English teacher. By your miracles, I was mysteriously discharged from military service and was in the reeducation camp for only a short time—shorter than that of any other officer of my former military school. My family moved to a rural village and lived in poverty. As my solemn vow, I will serve you from now until my death. Please help me to complete my promises to you, and take us safely to the United States of America. I pray in the Name of the Lord Jesus Christ. Amen!"

I wanted to go to the United States to live, while having only prayers to go on. My prayers were based on the book of Samuel Morris, an American tribal prince in Liberia whose tribal name was Prince Kaboo. Kaboo was imprisoned after a fierce bloody battle in which his tribe was defeated. He was tied to a tree in the jungle, and one night an extreme light shined on him and untied him, setting him free. He ran to a village where American missionaries were teaching new believers. He joined them and converted to Christianity. He was willing to go to New York to learn about the Holy Spirit. He prayed for three days and nights, asking the Lord to command the captain to allow him to embark on the journey. Two sailors who were meant to board the ship never showed, and the captain immediately let Kaboo replace them.

Kaboo went to the United States through his prayers and by God's miracles. My journey was similar, as I too came to the United States through prayers and by His miracles. Kaboo later became a student of a Bible college, as did I. Kaboo died at that college having not finished his education, while I could have died but would live on to serve the Lord.

Section V

My Thanksgiving for God's Miracles

Chapter 20
Mission in the Refugee Camps

In Thailand

After a long night at sea, all of the Vietnamese refugees were feeling much better. We ate three meals a day each day we were on the ship. The sailors prepared meals and brought them to us at the stern of the ship. We didn't have to do anything but relax. I took advantage of our free time and held a worship service on the ship. Everyone was invited—believers and nonbelievers. I asked everyone to sit, and I opened the service, saying, "Ladies and gentlemen, praise the Lord for the safety we now have on the *Leslie Lykes* as we make our way to Thailand. It took our small old wooden boat less than two days to be picked up. Was it an accident? Was it luck? Was it by our good means? Was it excellent navigation? No, it was not. I can tell you that we would all be at the bottom of the ocean, a delicious meal for the sharks, if the ship had not come in time to rescue us."

I held up the Bible and asked, "Do you know this book? This is the Bible I brought with me from Vietnam. I read it and based my prayers on its words for the past three months. Let me read a passage from the book of Psalms, chapter 107, verses 23–32: 'Those who go down in ships, who do business on great waters; they have seen the works of the Lord, and His wonders in the deep. For He spoke and raised up a stormy wind, which lifted up the waves of the sea. They rose up to the heavens, they went down to the depths; their soul melted away in their misery. They reeled and staggered like a drunken man, and were at their wits' end. Then they cried to the Lord in their trouble, and He brought them out of their distresses. He caused the storm to be still, so that the waves of the sea were hushed. Then they were glad because they were quiet, so He guided them to their desired haven. Let them give thanks to the Lord for His loving kindness, and for His wonders to the sons of men! Let them extol Him also in the congregation of the people, and praise Him at the seat of the elders.'

"Did you know that I had a vision from God about our trip? He encouraged me to depart with you all." I retold them the vision God had given me and told them of my prayers for our safety. I said to them, "We are now safe on this ship, and to whom shall we give our thanks? The Lord Jesus Christ, that is God, is whom we give our thanks to. He is the Creator—powerful, omnipotent, omnipresent, and omniscient. The Lord God is powerful, can do anything, can be everywhere, and can know everything."

I suggested we praise the Lord in song, and we sang together the popular hymn "How Great Thou Art." After we sang, I prayed, "Oh, dear Lord, Jesus Christ, we are thankful that you sent this ship to rescue us. Without your help, we would be in the stomachs of sharks. We ask you to take us to the United States safely. I pray in the name of our Lord, Jesus Christ. Amen!" When the service was over, I saw Mr. Blaine Buckley, the ship's first mate, standing beside one of our men. He was weeping and said the hymn reminded him of his family, whom he missed greatly.

It took the ship two more days to reach Thailand, and when we finally arrived, we needed to remain onboard for processing. I was called to enter the ship's cabin, where the captain and a Thai colonel from the Thai Department of the Interior were waiting with a civilian interpreter. First they asked the captain about his personal details and then about the boat rescue. They asked about the kind of boat we were on, our race, the reason he picked us up, and when and where the rescue occurred. He explained that he had picked us up for moral reasons. He then asked me similar questions. I told him that forty-seven Vietnamese refugees had been on a wooden boat to seek political protection.

After the interview, they had each person complete a form permitting him or her to enter Thailand. A *Bangkok Post* newspaper reporter also came to interview the captain and several others on the ship. On the morning of October 8, 1980, we all asked to prepare to leave the ship and enter Thailand. The police ships were ready to take us to the mainland, where we would gather and wait for orders. I asked for a moment to express my thanks and said, "Dear ship captain, first mate, sailors, and passengers on the *Leslie Lykes*, On behalf of the forty-seven Vietnamese refugees, I would like to express our heartfelt thanks and deep gratitude for the rescue, clothes, money, and courtesy during our stay. Without your love and help, we all would have died at sea. We pray that the Lord God bless you, your ship, your families, and your country for your good deeds. Please forgive us for what we have done wrong during our stay on your ship. Thank you."

Everyone clapped their hands, and some people cried when they saw us leave them for the police ships. As we walked toward the police ships, I looked with love and appreciation toward the ship's staff and all the people who were standing there. While the police ships were taking us to the mainland, some of the refugees cried, thinking of the captain and all the seamen, and their love and kindness to us. They had been so nice to us poor refugees, helping us with all their hearts. The Thailand government and people, who permitted us to reside in their country until we found permanent locations, also touched us. We thanked the Lord God for bringing us safely to the *Leslie Lykes* and to Thailand for all of us to have a good future.

The police ships took all of us to the mainland of Thailand and transferred us to the team of the United Nations High Commissioner for Refugees (UNHCR) personnel. That team was composed of three persons—one man and two women—who spoke English. They put us on two passenger buses, which departed quickly. They stopped on the road in front of a restaurant to eat dinner, but we remained on the bus. Perhaps they wanted to ensure none of us escaped. After mealtime, they had the bus driver head toward the refugee camp. I did not know where the bus was going, but it took us a very long time to get to the camp from the departure place. When the bus arrived at the camp, it was midnight. I told my people not to say anything, because we were staying at a strange place, but to let me cope with problems if they came about.

The Leamsing Refugee Camp

The camp leader was a Thai captain who wore civilian clothes and spoke to us in Thai that was translated through a Vietnamese interpreter. The interpreter was also a refugee, about fifty years old. He spoke to me and gave us some old mosquito nets, blankets, and sleeping mats. We were separated into smaller groups by family. Everyone was soon sound asleep after the long day on the buses.

The next morning, a loudspeaker woke us, telling me that as the representative for the people, I needed to see an American interviewer. It was still early in the morning, about 7:00 a.m. I didn't have any pants to wear, so my wife's niece Kim Anh gave me her pants to temporarily put on for this urgent interview. I met an American, his secretary, and a Vietnamese interpreter. I saluted everyone there, and the interviewer showed me a chair to sit in. After he realized I could speak English well, he dismissed the interpreter.

He explained that honesty was important in the interview and that I would not be able to resettle in the United States if I lied to him. He started out with some questions about my personal life regarding my education, occupation, marriage, children, reason for traveling overseas, etc. For an hour, I answered his questions about my life. Before he dismissed me, he said he would come back the next day to ask me more questions. When he returned the next day, he shook my hand and acknowledged that all I had told him the day prior was true. He now had additional questions about our boat, the people, and our trip from Vietnam. Since the memories were still so fresh, it was easy for me to recount the story. My answers satisfied his questions, and when the interview was over, he put his book and pen in his briefcase and said, "Your resettlement will not be a problem at all; it should be very quick. During your stay here, if there is anything you dislike or someone hurts you, immediately come and see this man." He pointed toward a man nearby, and his words encouraged me during our stay in the camp.

When I first saw Southern Baptist Convention (SBC) missionary Rev. D. K. coming to the chapel for mail delivery to the refugees, I met him and said that we were the Vietnamese Christians who had just arrived there one day ago. I asked him if he had a few minutes for me to speak about the refugees. He agreed, and at the next worship service on Sunday, he reserved a special time for me to preach to the service. I did not preach but spoke to the refugees, saying, "My dear ladies and gentlemen, I would like to say that we are now safe in this country. We no longer see the ocean, but mainland with the Thai and Vietnamese people. Like I said to you on the ship *Leslie Lykes*, God's miracles brought us safely to this country and prepared us to go to the United States as free people. Our presence here was not accidental but was rather a miracle. As you see, our boat was lost, and we were finally found, far from the Vietnam coastal area, thanks to the ship's first mate, Blaine Buckley. We had no shortage of food or water.

"Do you know that I prayed to the Lord Jesus Christ, asking him for three things? One: that no one would be lost from the various canoes. Two: that we would safely pass through the heavy rain that fell on us and that it would end when we arrived at the ocean. And three: that an American ship would pick us up.

"Three things were fulfilled: One: forty-seven people; twenty-four men, thirteen women, and ten children were safely taken to the boat by the various canoes. Two: a heavy rain was pouring on us continually till we arrived safely at the ocean. And three: an American merchant vessel named the *Leslie Lykes* came to pick us up at 5:00 p.m. on October 5, 1980.

"The Lord sent a ship to rescue us in response to my prayers. Otherwise, we might have been food for the sharks some days ago. The Lord Jesus Christ not only wants to rescue our boat, our physical bodies, but He also wants to save our souls. If you agree with me that the Lord rescued us, you should accept Him as your personal Savior.

"If you accept Him as your personal Savior, just raise your hands as a sign of your acceptance. I see almost everyone raising their hands, so I invite you to come up to the pulpit and kneel down for Rev. D. K. to pray for you."

Most of my people came to the pulpit and knelt down, and Rev. DK prayed in Vietnamese for them. Since that day, they faithfully attended the worship service twice a week, Thursday and Sunday at the chapel. After taking a few days off, I began working every day with the church as a Bible teacher focusing on baptism. I also worked for the American Embassy's office at the refugee camp as an interpreter and the UNHCR as the director of the English language school. They paid me ten bahts (fifty US cents) a day when we worked with either JVA or UNHCR. I was busy managing the refugees who were participating in activities with Rev. D. K. and was teaching the Bible to those who planned to be baptized by immersion.

Rev. D. K. loved me and wanted to introduce me to a mission pastor of a Vietnamese church in Oklahoma. I gave him my résumé so he could mail it to any church that might be interested in me. One morning, we were all addressed on the loudspeaker and told that all forty-seven refugees would be leaving for Panatnikhom Transit Center. We were all joyful, but Rev. D. K. was sad and said, "I didn't expect you all to leave for the United States, because I really love you and need you to help me make this chapel full of Christians. But I cannot do anything against God's will. I pray and wish that you all can go to the United States very quickly. I hope to see you soon. May the Lord bless you at Panatnikhom Transit Center."

Panatnikhom Transit Center

We were taken to Panatnikhom Transit Center—with the exception of brother Luan and his nephew, who were headed to Indonesia, and two others, whose relatives were living in Germany. We were at the camp from December of 1980 to January of 1981. The camp was built on a hill without trees and was quite hot. The houses were made with sheet metal walls and roofs, and with windows but no doors, so it was very hot. When we first arrived, I was hired to work for the JVA again at the same wages. My daughters worked for a Thai restaurant near our lodging and earned twenty Thai bahts per day. I found a job for my wife where she earned ten bahts per day. So everyone in our household was employed near the transit center.

We celebrated Christmas of 1980 in Thailand. I set up a room in our lodge and held a simple program to preach to a few attendants. We had nothing to eat that evening, owing to our refugee situation, but the Lord understood our needs.

As the JVA interpreter, I had the opportunity to help several families. For example, in the Leamsing camp, a man and his wife fought. Neither of them was allowed to go to the United States. Unfortunately, the husband was the boat leader, who registered with the local government to leave the Vietnamese coastal area. When he came to the refugee camp, he secretly united with another woman. This caused his wife to be jealous. I described the misunderstanding between the wife and her husband to the JVA and asked them to let the kids go to the United States for their education. Keeping the kids at the camp simply caused the camp to be crowded and created bitterness among the family. It was decided that the whole family would be allowed to go to the United States for a short time.

In Panatnikhom Transit Center, a mother with five children had been there for several months while her husband was kept in Singapore, unable to leave. He had a plane ticket to resettle in Italy but refused to go because his wife was going to the United States. His wife was also waiting for her husband, so she was unable to go to the United States as well. The husband and wife were kept separated for a long time in waiting. She came to me for help. I presented an application to the UNHCR and asked them to help resolve the situation. Her entire family was called to prepare to go the United States. She was so joyful that they could be reunited.

Those were typical of the stories I was involved in. I also had evangelistic talks with refugees about God's love and salvation.

Many people came to me to discuss the differences between Catholicism and Evangelical doctrine, as well as to understand why there was a battle between the Catholics and Protestants in Europe in ancient times.

I was in the refugee camp for only three and half months, but I did my best to help the refugees whenever possible. I saw a lot of professional missionaries of various denominations come to help as well. I believe I was allowed to stay there to help the refugees know God and find salvation. I praised the Lord for their interest in Bible study and that they joyfully accepted the Lord Jesus Christ as their Savior. They came to the United States and lived there for over thirty-three years and continued to follow the Lord Jesus. Some of them now serve in the ministry as senior pastors, church pianists, medical doctors serving the Lord as bivocational pastors, and active deacons. I seldom meet up with them, because the country is so large, but I still hear about their faithfulness as Christians.

Chapter 21

Christian Ministry in the United States

In California

While we were still in the camp, an announcement was posted on the refugee board for people that were set to leave for the United States. I was so happy to see the names of my family on the list! Our final destination was listed as Los Angeles, California. We were taken to Lumbini city to stay for one day before going to Bangkok Airport. We went through an orientation on visa laws, passports, refugee documents, baggage, children, sickness, security checkpoints, etc. The night before we left, I was so excited and peaceful, thinking that all the suffering we experienced would end here in Thailand. That night felt like a critical moment between the past and the future. I reflected on the events of the past, many of which were full of sorrow and worry, which brought me to tears.

The next day would be a great day for my whole family; we would begin a new period of life full of lively activities. Refugees like us would have the opportunity, by God's mercy and grace, to switch from hostility to hospitality, bitterness to gentility, and anxiety to peace. The captain's voice came over the loudspeaker and announced that we would be leaving for San Francisco's airport.

We were warmly greeted by a group of Vietnamese volunteers in San Francisco when we arrived at the gate. They took us to the hotel where we would stay overnight before continuing on to Los Angeles the next day. We had a dinner of familiar Vietnamese dishes. It was very simple, but it was also very delicious to us, as we had not had such dishes since we left Vietnam. One of my former students, N. T. Chau, was staying in the same hotel with her college friend, as San Francisco was her final destination. They both accepted the Lord Jesus Christ as their personal Savior that night after they heard me tell them of God's love and the miracle he performed in getting us to the United States safely.

The next day, our family was taken back to the airport for our connecting flight to Los Angeles, California. It took the small plane less than an hour to get us there. When we arrived at the gate, a Vietnamese Buddhist monk, who seemed to be staring at us in a dissatisfied manner, met us. He asked "Are you a Christian?"

I promptly answered, "Yes."

He asked me when I became a Christian, and I told him that I had been one since my boyhood in 1947.

It turns out he had seen the Vietnamese Bible in the straw basket I was carrying. He wasn't pleased to take us, but he took us to his small car and drove to a pagoda in Los Angeles. I gave him the address of my wife's older brother so that we could head that way. Using his phone, we phoned him, and I talked to my wife's nephew, telling him the pagoda's address. The nephew's pastor came to pick us up about a half hour later. He was Rev. Hien, the Vietnamese Evangelical Church pastor of Hawthorne. My wife's brother and his wife met us when we arrived at their home. We stayed there for a week, and then we rented another house for many people to live together. The house was located on the same street as my wife's brother's. While the rent was $500 a month, we were able to split that among the many people living with us.

The next day, my wife's brother took our family to get our medical checkups, Social Security cards, skin tests, welfare declarations, and everything else that we needed to get established. I wanted to work instead of receive welfare benefits, even though I was eligible since my youngest children were less than ten years old. I accepted a job at the Medical Optics Center, where I looked at little bottles of soft contact lenses to ensure there were no broken lenses. I had worked there for about three months when the daughter of some friends of ours invited me to visit other factories to ask for a position with better wages. I visited a factory, and while I was speaking to the guard, a manager was listening nearby. He asked me if I wanted to work there, and I said yes. He hired me right away because I knew English and could translate for the other employees if necessary. I started at just five dollars per hour, but I believed that was good enough. A woman who was in charge of supervising our group was very serious and strict. I always did what she told me to do, though, although I felt there was some discrimination occurring.

An associate pastor suggested I teach a men's Sunday school class. I was elected to serve the Lord as the men's club director as well. Rev. Pham, a former missionary to the highlanders in central Vietnam and current senior pastor for the Vietnamese Evangelical Church in Long Beach, came with his wife to our home and spoke to me about becoming the Vietnamese Christian Missionary Alliance (CMA) minister in the United States. While it was good for me to hear, there was no organizational support offered to me at that time.

By January 1981, we had been living in the United States for one year and had managed to save $570 from a whole year of labor and our welfare earnings. We had only my income to count on and a six-member family to provide for. We were crowded in our one-person apartment, and the relationship between my family and my wife's relatives was becoming a little strained in such close quarters.

We met another Christian family, whose hometown was Vinh Long, South Vietnam. Their father knew me from when he came to Soc Trang to sell pocket-sized books of the four Gospels. He used to stay at the church when he was in the area. His older brother, Rev. Nguyen—a missionary to Laos, current chairman of the Vietnamese Evangelical Church of Europe, and popular preacher and theological writer in Paris, France—had been my former classmate in a Bible class in Vinh Long in 1960.

We agreed to meet them every Wednesday night in their home at 7:30 p.m. for a Bible study. The friendship between their son Dan and our daughter Phuong developed, which led to a love and their future marriage. It also gave us the idea to move our family to another place for a better life. We decided to start our move right after Phuong's engagement with Dan in April of that year. Phuong's engagement ceremony was very simple, held in the presence of two families in my one-room apartment on a Saturday morning in Inglewood, California. Through a mutual friend, we met Mrs. K. B., a government social worker in Fort Smith, Arkansas, and decided to move to Fort Smith, as the cost of living was lower there. We said good-bye to my wife's family. Dan Nguyen, who used to live in Fort Smith, drove my family to Arkansas that month.

In Arkansas

Our 1970 Chevrolet left the crowded Californian city early in the morning. We prayed before starting the engine, and Dan drove us on our way. Arkansas was a state of chicken farms, providing many of the chickens for the United States. It was also an evangelical church state, President Bill Clinton's home state, and now our new home.

Since we prayed before our departure, the move was relatively smooth; we had only some minor problems with the radiator and transmission. We stopped in Albuquerque, New Mexico, to rest overnight in a motel. We all stayed in one room, but it was comfortable and warm. The next day was a nice day in Albuquerque, which encouraged us on our journey. Dan took us into the central city and stopped in the front yard of Mrs. K. B.'s house. We stayed with her for one week and then found our own home to rent. Dan and I found a home with two rooms for $150 per month. It was near Spark Hospital and had a very large yard for the children to play in. Mrs. K. B. took Dan to find a job, and he was hired at a milk production company in central city. My wife, eldest daughter, and I got jobs at the Specialty Poultry Company in Van Buren, the neighboring city to Fort Smith. We were earning $3.50 per hour, working eight hours a day, five days a week; the means were stable for the whole family. Our other children were in school; Loan was in high school, and Ai and Linh were in elementary school. We joined the Vietnamese Southside Baptist Church, where Rev. Nguyen served as pastor. He has since gone to be with the Lord.

One morning in April, Rev. J. F., his wife, and another woman from Grand Avenue Baptist Church came to my house for an Evangelism Explosion visit. We welcomed them in, and I told them about our faith in Christ and our boat rescue. Rev. J. F. said, "For a long time, we have really prayed for a leader like you in our Vietnamese congregation. I believe the Lord sent you to us as an answer! You can preach to the Vietnamese congregation next month, on May 2." He gave me his business card with the date May 2, 1982, on it.

The following Sunday was May 2, and a church deacon came to pick us up and take us to the church chapel. The chapel was the former sanctuary for a six-hundred-member congregation that had moved to a newly built sanctuary. Instead of preaching, I gave my testimony on our boat rescue at sea. One lady spoke to me on behalf of the Vietnamese executive committee and asked me to be their pastor. I told her that her call was precious but I needed time to ask God's will. After a month of praying about it, I accepted their invitation to enter the ministry as the mission pastor at Grand Avenue Baptist Church in Fort Smith, Arkansas. I was interviewed by the senior pastor and then voted on by the American and Vietnamese congregations on June 6, 1982. I began my ministry at their church that very day, almost two years from the day we were rescued at sea. It was a miracle that God allowed these two congregations to approve me and let me begin a new ministry of service to God.

The American church apparently loved me, because more Vietnamese joined the Vietnamese congregation through baptism. So many people joined that the senior pastor, Dr. J. B., spoke to the deacons and said that the congregation admired me for the growth in the church, and that I had baptized more people than had been baptized in the American congregation. The deacons decided to increase my salary, and after two years of ministry, I was officially ordained. Dr. J. B. encouraged me to attend seminary to improve my knowledge of the Bible. I applied to Southwestern Baptist Theological Seminary and was accepted. A few American pastors from the rural cities joined me as we carpooled to Shawnee, Oklahoma, every Monday. I was also admitted to study at West Ark Community College to take English composition courses.

In August of 1982, our first daughter, Phuong Minh Lam, and Dan Hong Nguyen married in the chapel. Rev. J. F. performed the ceremony, and a wedding banquet was held in the activities building. Phuong gave birth to three children. The first one was a daughter, Jennifer. The second was a son, John, who died when he was just one month old. The third was a daughter, Stephanie.

In Virginia

In April 1987, a layman from the Vietnamese Gospel Baptist Church in Alexandria, Virginia, called me to preach at his church. I accepted his invitation and visited the Washington, DC, area while the cherry blossoms were blooming. I was taken to First Baptist Church of Alexandria on King Street for the evening Saturday service, and I was quite surprised by the low attendance. Only four members and seven guests from another church were in attendance. I thought that perhaps the busy city life caused the church members to lack time to attend.

At the Sunday service, seventeen people attended, which showed me that this was a very weak church. The church members looked sad, and some of them asked me if I could be their pastor. I loved them because they were few and they did not receive any financial support from any organizations. I don't want to compare the two churches, but the Fort Smith church was experiencing great economic conditions and had three hundred Vietnamese members and three thousand American members, while the church in Alexandria had nothing.

I thought of our Lord Jesus Christ's ministry and how he began with nothing. I told them that if 100 percent of them voted to invite me there, it would attract me to move to Alexandria to serve. I returned to Fort Smith, but two weeks later they called me and invited me to serve with a 100 percent vote. They did not tell me details regarding salary, lodging arrangements, medical insurance, or moving expenses. Two of my children opposed my intention to move, and the church executive committee came to my house and asked me to stay. The senior pastor expressed his sadness for my resignation, embraced me with tears rolling down his cheek, and said, "Minh, I need you. Stay with me!"

I thought of a statement I had heard a church member claimed: "The majority of church growth was done by me, because I helped these people in many ways." I realized my stay at the Fort Smith church was unnecessary, as the other church really needed me. Through prayers and careful consideration, I decided to move, despite all the difficulty ahead, as I believed this was the vision the Lord had for me.

Prior to our move, our second daughter, Loan Phuong Lam, and Tuyen Van Nguyen were wedded. Dr. J. B. performed the ceremony in June 1987. After their wedding, they moved to Pittsburg, Pennsylvania, to continue their education.

After their departure, we also left Fort Smith, Arkansas, for Virginia. The church in Fort Smith grew from seventy members to three hundred by my fifth year, in 1987. I bought a used six-cylinder Pontiac for Ai, our sixteen-year-old son, so he could drive from Arkansas to Virginia. It took us two days to reach Virginia, with a one-night stay in Tennessee to rest for an evening. The next day, Ai drove the rest of the way until we reached Fredericksburg, Virginia, where we stopped at our relative's house to stay for a week. It was hard for us to find an apartment to live in, but a missionary pastor for the Mount Vernon Baptist Association introduced us to Bren Mar Apartments on Edsall Road, where the former pastor of the Vietnamese church of Alexandria used to live. Our application to rent an apartment there was accepted with help from the apartment manager, who was also Baptist.

The church gathered on a Sunday to discuss the salary, and they shared it with me only when the association director, Dr. W. C. told them to. The treasurer, Miss K. T. Tran, told me not to deposit the check until the Sunday service offerings were put in the church account. After they met, I realized there was no harmony here, but only division among them.

Another problem was that the committee members all lived quite far from the church and no one was friendly with each other. The previous pastor had left during the night without saying good-bye to any of the committee members, and another pastor had resigned right at the pulpit after only four months. I knew this had contributed to the state that the committee was now in.

The people in the area had to work hard to earn money and were too busy to come to church and work on their spiritual lives. Day by day, they missed the Bible lessons and sermons in worship. They ignored the church and easily forgot God, just like the sermons of Moses recorded in the book of Deuteronomy. Our family was making time for church and work. My wife was working at the printing factory, and Ai and Linh worked after school to contribute financially to the family.

The church did grow over time, demonstrating God's work and mercy despite the arguments, disagreements, division, and jealousy among the deacons. My ministry lasted two years, with success and frustration. One day I came with Rev. T. C. Ly to the Washington Bible College (WBC) and Capital Bible Seminar in Lanham, Maryland, to find a place for the 1988 Vietnamese National Baptist Conference. Rev. Ly was a master of arts student at the college, and I was interested in continuing my education. I promptly enrolled for the spring 1989 semester. I told the new executive committee about my full-time Bible education and decided that if they opposed my study, I would quit my pastorate. They not only agreed but also donated $1,600 for the first semester's tuition. I also attended the Community College of Annandale and Alexandria for forty hours of general education that I could transfer to the Washington Bible College. I graduated from the WBC with a BA in biblical study in 1993, a master of divinity from the Capital Bible Seminary in 1995, and a doctor of ministry from the Liberty Baptist Theological Seminary in 1998, when I was fifty-nine years old.

The Establishment of a New Church

The members of the Vietnamese congregation predominantly came to the United States through a few venues: American-Asian parentage (e.g., the father was American, the mother Vietnamese), marriage, the Orderly Departure Program (ODP), and the Humanity Operation (HO). They were often helped when they arrived, as everything was new and strange to them. They had to learn new languages, occupations, cultures, climates, religions, laws, customs, educational practices, and more, as everything was new. They went to church and gradually became Christians. They made friends with other churches or churchgoers and asked for help. They had an interest in the American holidays, the Bible, and studying Christ's birth, death, resurrection, and especially the topic of salvation.

From the beginning of 1994, chaos really ensued at the church for two major reasons. Jealousy was the first reason. Several new Christians joined the church, and they were elected by the congregation to serve as the executive committee. This group was then blamed for forming a religious party that sided with the pastor. The second reason was that my youngest daughter and the son of a deacon were in a relationship that ended badly. This caused a rebellious group to form and accuse me of creating church problems. A meeting was held with an American missionary present, and as a result, I resigned after my eight years of service.

I had intentions of moving to San Diego, California, to serve a church there, but several believers of the Alexandria congregation suggested that some new believers may not yet have the commitment to continue being faithful. So I decided that if

I left the area, all my work here would be in vain. We decided we should find a new church in the area so those who chose to do so could stay with us. We established a new church named Vietnamese Hope Baptist Church, a member of the Southern Baptist Convention that temporarily met in the Sunset Hills Baptist Church facilities. We held our first worship service on Sunday November 5, 1995. It seemed to grow like a young tree covered in green leaves, with God's mercy and miracles surrounding it. In 1996, fifty-six new believers joined the church by baptism. Nine years later, the church now has 450 members.

In June 2004, I was in a car accident. The chiropractor recommended I move to a warm climate to help my back. My wife and I moved to an old house in the city of Holiday, near Tampa, Florida. This was our first move without any children, as Ai and Linh stayed in Northern Virginia. Rev. Truong drove a U-Haul containing our clothes and books. A twelve-member church nearby needed me to be their pastor, so I accepted the position at $1,200/month. I was choosing to serve the Lord with an unhealthy body at the age of sixty-five.

Chapter 22

The Tenth Miracle: Christian Educational Improvement

Resignation or Educational Improvement?

Prior to leaving for Tampa, Florida, I had worked to improve my education. I believe I was able to accomplish this at my age only through God's miracles. As I mentioned earlier, I had gone to the Capital Bible Seminary in 1987 to see if we could hold the 1988 Vietnamese National Baptist Conference there. I had originally no intentions of returning to school, as financing and time presented challenges to me. However, I believed the Lord wanted me to attend that school to gain a stable background in the Scripture. In 1989, I was feeling troubled and a little depressed about the challenges we were facing at the church in Alexandria, so I decided to submit an application for enrollment. Since the church decided to pay for that first semester, it eased the financial burden, and the remaining semesters were discounted by half because I was a senior pastor.

The BA in biblical study was not hard for me to obtain, as I began my formal education already familiar with the stories, expositions, meanings, and background. After I graduated in 1993, I took a two-week trip to the Holy Land, organized by the

Washington Bible College staff. I was admitted into the Master of Divinity program automatically, as I had already completed a degree at the school. I completed the program in 1995—in two years instead of three, as I had tested out of some of the courses in my earlier program. I intended to stop there, as I had already labored six years in school, but my wife pushed me to try to obtain the last piece, my doctorate. I applied to Liberty University's Liberty Baptist Theological Seminary. Two weeks later, the Admissions Department called and told me I had been accepted into the Doctor of Ministry program for the summer session.

I drove three hours on Route 29 to Lynchburg every weekend and stayed at the Econo Lodge Hotel five days a week, Monday through Friday. After I attended the classes, I spent three months on the course paper and submitted it for grading. I took eight classes in that fashion, earning twenty-four credits with B+ and A grades. I then wrote a thesis statement and reasoning, and I submitted it to the dean for approval. With the dean's approval, I had to submit chapters on a timely basis to my sponsor, the president of the American Association of Christian Counselors.

When I finished my thesis draft, titled "Ministering to the Vietnamese Christian Troubled Families in the United States of America," I sent three copies to my sponsor, and he sent them on to examiners. The thesis council examiners consisted of three American scholars: a doctor of psychology, a doctor of education, and a doctor of theology. They asked many questions regarding Vietnamese culture, philosophy, and education, as well as the refugee way of life. The questions were not too challenging, and they agreed to provide a good rating if I corrected what they wanted changed. The dean's secretary typed up their request and sent it to me within thirty minutes.

On that three-hour drive home, I was thinking of my upcoming graduation. I submitted the corrections that had been requested, and the following week an examiner phoned me and congratulated me on my upcoming graduation from Liberty University. I was so happy to receive this call! I praised the Lord for my education and graduation at fifty-nine years old! Fifty people from my church and the Vietnamese Baptist Church of Clifton Park in Silver Spring, Maryland, packed into many cars, buses, and vans to attend my graduation in Lynchburg, Virginia, on May 9, 1998. Tears filled my eyes as I approached the state to receive my diploma from Dr. Jerry Falwell, president of Liberty University. I thought of my parents being uneducated but working hard to bring up eight children and of how proud they would be seeing me earn my doctorate.

It was such a miracle that God let me patiently follow my education in my old age. I had burdened both family and church. If God had not helped me, I would not have completed my educational dreams. Praise the Lord for His love, grace, compassion, and miracles.

In Tampa, Florida

Our house in Tampa, Florida, was almost an hour away from the church we joined. Twelve people, including Rev. Truong, my driver; my wife; and I, attended our first Sunday worship service. We met in the Nazarene Church for worship and some activities. Our church was nondenominational, and we called it The Vietnamese Hope Gospel Church.

Praise the Lord for His blessings as the church grew so fast. In just nine months, we had sixty-seven people attending worship. We held three services a week: a Wednesday-evening prayer service, a Friday-evening Bible study, and a Sunday-morning Bible study and worship. Some people joined us from neighboring churches, and church members invited others. The executive committee and church members were quite encouraged by our growth.

My wife and I developed a hobby of planting trees and vegetables during our short stay in Tampa. We bought some fruit trees at the flea market and grew them in our back and front yards. It was very interesting to see the new flowers and fruits appear among the trees every morning.

The church members really seemed to enjoy seeing the beach, having baptisms on the beach, and enjoying picnics at the beach. There were a lot of beautiful beaches in southern Florida, but our favorite aspect from our time there was the Friday night Bible study. For twenty nights, sixteen of us gathered at Mr. Nguyen's house to spend quality time together studying the book of Revelation. We mined God's Word together, and it gave me such an appreciation for the diligence needed to understand God's treasure.

An aging man, the former South Vietnamese Army full colonel Mr. Nguyen previously had wept on only two occasions: his mother's funeral and General Hieu Van Nguyen's historic death in 1975. He wept a third time when I gave my resignation to leave the Tampa area. In response to his emotion, I told him that we were called to establish a new church for the Vietnamese people in Austin, Texas. I was sorrowful when I left them for the nonbelievers.

Our house was put up for sale or rent in Tampa when we left for Texas. I rented a U-Haul for Rev. Truong to drive us to Austin in November 2005. It took us almost a day to arrive, and Tuyen Van Nguyen, my son-in-law, was waiting in front of the house he and my second daughter had purchased for us to live in.

My wife fell down in front of the house some days later while walking to the trash can. We didn't know it at the time but would come to find out that was an indicator of Parkinson's. We would learn more about that a few years later.

I seemed to move from place to place in my life, indicating a mobile destiny that I had experienced since my first position in Soc Trang. Between 1965 and 1981, I moved five times, all over parts of Vietnam and to the United States. I felt a lot like the Prophet Elijah, who moved from place to place according to the book of 1 Kings. He moved from Tishbite, Gilead, to the brook Cherith, east of Jordan; then from Cherith to Zarephath, Sidon; from Zarephath to Mount Carmel, where there was a meeting of the prophets of Baal against the prophet Elijah; from Mount Carmel to the brook KIshon; then back to Mount Carmel one more time. He ran from Mount Carmel to reach Jezreel before Ahab. Finally he ran from Jezreel to Beersheba, and from there to the wilderness at a juniper tree. After a long rest, he walked forty days and nights to Horeb, the mount of God. From Mount Horeb, he went to the wilderness of Damascus to anoint Hazael king over Aram, Jehu the son of Nimshi king of Israel, and Elisha the son of Shaphat of Abel-meholah as prophet in his place.

Since coming to the United States of America in 1981, we have moved from Hawthorne to Inglewood, California; Inglewood to Fort Smith, Arkansas; Fort Smith to Alexandria, Virginia; from Alexandria to Burke, Virginia; from Burke to Annandale, Virginia; from Annandale to Holiday, Florida; from Holiday to Austin, Texas; from Austin to Annandale, Virginia; from Annandale to Pensacola, Florida; from Pensacola to Annandale, Virginia; from Annandale to Orlando, Florida; and from Orlando to Annandale, Virginia. We moved eleven times in thirty-three years, from 1981 to 2014. The Lord was with us through all those moves and kept our trips free of vehicle malfunctions, accidents, traffic law violations, and sickness.

Our move reminded me of our movement in the little old wooden boat on the Pacific Ocean as we traveled to the big ship for a rescue. The Lord was definitely with us to protect us from danger, just as He protected Israel when they moved to the Promised Land with a pillar of cloud by day and a pillar of fire by night. (See Exodus 13:21.) "When you pass through the waters, I will be with you; and through the rivers, they will not overflow you. When you walk through the fire, you will not scorch, nor will the flame burn you" (Isaiah 43:2). "Then they cried to the Lord in their trouble, and He brought them out of their distresses. He caused the storm to be still, so that the waves of the sea were hushed. Then they were glad because they were quiet so He guided them to their desired haven" (Psalm 107:28–30).

When you read the Bible, do not think that the old stores are no longer effective and applicable to today. The Lord still performs great things for His children as a response to prayers, just as He did for the Israelites. Scripture tells us so: "Jesus Christ is the same yesterday and today and forever" (Hebrews 13:8). During my prayers, I believe the Lord Jesus Christ is near me, just as He was beside Hannah to hear her prayers. (See 1 Samuel 1:10–11.) I believe serious prayers from Christians with faith in the Lord are like requests from an applicant's hand submitted directly to the powerful receiver, who is glad to give the answer.

In Austin, Texas

We came to Austin to live near my daughter Loan Phuong Nguyen and her husband, Tuyen Van Nguyen, with their children, Deborah Quynh Nguyen and Dylan Nam Nguyen. Tuyen worked for IBM, Loan worked for an elementary school, and their children were in elementary school.

Our home was within walking distance of theirs, and we held our first church service at Tuyen's house at 11:00 a.m. on January 1, 2006. Two old women, Loan's family, and my family attended worship; we were eight people in total. I played the mandolin, and five people sang Vietnamese hymns. The next week, Tuyen and I went to see the director of the Austin Baptist Association (ABA), Dr. Smith, so our new church could join the ABA. Dr. Smith also found some churches to help us during our installation.

Our two families worked very hard evangelizing every day of the week, including holidays. We gradually grew to twenty-five members and Gateway Baptist Church agreed to let us use their facilities, rent-free. Several new believers were baptized at the church, and they encouraged us to be more evangelistic.

A Heart Disease Became Normal

I visited a cardiologist once a month for the atrial fibrillation caused by the car accident I had in June 2004. The injury to my back caused the condition, which resulted in me taking Coumadin once a day and getting blood tests done once a month. One day after my EKG was conducted, the doctor came running in and said, "Normal, normal! Praise the Lord for a miracle!" He told me that the atrial fibrillation was gone. I still needed to come see him once a month to ensure it didn't return. I was very thankful for God's miracles.

Since the church had been established from nothing, my salary came from my son-in-law's tithe of $900. The church had no financial support, so it was stable only by faith. I preached at some churches in Dallas, Texas, and taught at the Vietnamese Baptist Theological Institute. Several American Baptist Churches in the ABA invited me to preach at churches in rural areas. They loved our newly established church and provided financial support. Thanks to their support and that of others who donated money monthly, we grew continuously until we averaged about fifty people every Sunday. We were able to purchase property and a small house that we used for worship and Sunday school. I accepted a position at First Baptist Church of Pensacola, as the mission pastor to the Vietnamese congregation. Prior to moving to Pensacola, I invited Rev. Le to take my position as pastor, and he accepted. Rev. Truong drove our U-Haul safely to Pensacola in February 2007.

In Pensacola, Florida

I quickly purchased a brick three-bedroom, two-bath home with waterfront property in a nice community called Marcus Lake. A church member and his family who had come to help us move in met us. They finished moving all of our heavy things in a half hour, and then we shared a meal with them, as they had brought us dinner, knowing we would be too tired to prepare a meal after the long journey.

I presented to the pastor and my supervisor, Rev. Minton, for service. They welcomed me and had my office prepared with a new desk, chair, and computer. My supervisor told me the office hours I would work, which included some daily hospital visits during the week. They expected me to be at the office at 8:00 a.m., take an hour for lunch, and then come back and work until 5:00 p.m. I had thought that as the mission pastor, I would not stay in the office but rather reach out to as many nonbelievers as possible. So I asked if I could stay in the office in the mornings and conduct home visits in the afternoon, and they agreed. I often stopped by Mr. Sa's grocery on my way to church, just to catch up. I also drove to Mr. Nguyen home for prayer visits during his time with lung cancer.

Pensacola was a small city, but it had six hospitals because of the high aging population. The pastor of First Baptist Church said he had performed over one hundred funerals in the past two years for his church members. While it was a beautiful area, it was not a very active area for the Vietnamese church. I worked really hard to grow the congregation, but it did not seem to grow. The size of the room we met in was smaller than a classroom, located on the fourth floor, and didn't seem to help us attract people. Another reason for the slow growth was division among church members. A third reason was that the majority of the members were passive, seldom inviting friends to go to church. Lastly, the church members lived rather far from the church—at least three hours from the church building.

When my close friend Mr. Nguyen died from lung cancer in December 2007, I decided it was time for me to serve elsewhere. I planned to visit Vietnam for a month and then resign. However, there was a bit of a complication with the housing in Saigon. The house I built in Ban Co belonged to my wife's parents, but was this complicated in the passing of my wife's father. The youngest son received the house in the will, but his stepmother was the official resident of the home. He could not take possession of it, because she lived there; and she could not sell the house, because of the will. They both allowed me to take the house under the condition that I take care of her living arrangements financially. In 2008, she was seriously ill, so we went to help sell the house.

When we returned to the United States, I left the letter of resignation on Rev. Minton's desk. He asked me to announce my resignation to the Vietnamese congregation the following Sunday during service, with him present. Everyone seemed surprised at the announcement, but one church member wanted to rent my house, so we left in peace, believing it was God's will.

In Orlando, Florida

When I wrote the resignation letter, I was sixty-nine years old and decided it was time for me to retire from Christian ministry. I made a decision to return to Northern Virginia to live with two of my children, Ai and Linh. Rev. Truong flew to Pensacola to drive our U-Haul to Virginia, as he had done on all my former trips. Around the time that I resigned, I received news from the Vietnamese Baptist Church in Orlando, Florida, about the resignation of their pastor. I immediately thought that he would be a good fit for Pensacola, so I made some calls, and as a result, Pastor Uc accepted God's call to be the pastor in Pensacola. My promise to First Baptist Church of Pensacola was kept through him, and the current pastor remains active in that church to my knowledge.

While I had good intentions of retiring, the Lord had other plans. Several days after I arrived in Virginia, the Vietnamese Baptist Church of Orlando, Florida, called to invite me to preach at a revival meeting. I later learned that they planned to invite me to be their pastor, but they did not let me know that in advance. I went to Orlando and preached at an evening service. Two people accepted the Lord Jesus as their Savior that night. Between the service and the meal, the deacon chair took me to the pastor's office and said, "This is your office."

The statement surprised me, and the next morning another deacon of the church (a former Bible student of mine from ten years ago) told me that several church members had contacted him, expecting me to become their pastor. I thought this was impossible, because I intended to retire. Before the Sunday morning service, several women took me aside and told me they would like to invite me to be their pastor. I answered them by saying "I can't answer you now, because I don't know God's will or my wife's will. Let us pray before I give you an answer."

I worked hard that Sunday. After the morning service, there was a big luncheon for everyone. Afterward, the church wanted me to review the book of Revelation in an hour, which I did. After a fifteen-minute break, they wanted to discuss theology, and after that a deacon told me there would be a meeting with me after dinner. That night, twenty church members joined me for dinner at the house I was staying in. The chair deacon stood up and told me that he represented the whole church in asking me to serve as pastor. He asked me to say yes when called officially at the upcoming church conference.

I repeated my earlier answer—that I needed to know God's will and my wife's will. They told me another candidate was ready and willing, so I came back to Virginia to discuss it with my family. Two weeks later, the chair deacon called me to tell me that 100 percent of the church members had elected me to serve as pastor. It was hard for me to answer them, as my wife would not agree to come with me if I served in Orlando. She believed that since we had told the church in Pensacola we were retiring, they would be upset if I took another position. However, I prayed and believed that the Lord was not ready for me to retire yet, so I accepted the position. My wife didn't want to come, so I asked her to teach me to cook some simple meals and operate the washing machine and dryer. When she heard me ask these questions, she decided to follow me. I was so happy to hear her decision! We left for Virginia, with Rev. Truong driving our U-Haul again. This was the fifth time he drove long-distance for us. I sincerely appreciate my Christian friend's heart and his gift of helping. He was devoted and dedicated, which can be hard to come by.

We started our service to the Lord in Orlando in August 2008. The parsonage was located on the church grounds. The church had purchased property a year before, but it took on debt to do so. Our plan was to pay that debt off through the sale of recorded sermons and offerings collected from the church members.

The church grew through my time in service—so much so that the executive committee planned to enlarge the building and add an extra room for youth activities. The backyard was brightly landscaped, and we grew a vegetable garden to be used by the kitchen. The church members were very satisfied. We performed several baptisms of new believers, and I was invited to preach at the Vietnamese National Baptist Conference in Dallas, Texas, on July 4, 2009. A church member brought sermon CDs with her and raised $2,500 in sales. Praise the Lord for lowering the debt as much as possible!

The new believers getting baptized by Dr. Minh Van Lam at First Baptist Church in 2011.

Not long after that, my wife suddenly started falling on the ground more frequently when walking. I took her to several different doctors, Western and Oriental, but no one could determine the cause of her falling. She lost a significant amount of weight, going from 130 pounds to 90 pounds. She had difficulty sleeping at night and lost her sense of taste. She couldn't stay long at church, so she would listen to my sermon and then return home to lie in bed. She was unable to cook or do anything around the house. We would eat lunch at the restaurant and order meals to bring home for dinner. A group of women from church realized we needed help, and each family cooked meals for us and brought them over. How nice they were!

We did not know what the Lord wanted us to do—resign or stay and serve in Orlando. We learned of God's plan when our youngest daughter, Linh, came to visit with her family, not knowing of my wife's health problems.

Back to Alexandria, Virginia

When Linh visited us in March 2010, she wept upon seeing my wife so seriously ill. She took me aside to speak with me at the parsonage and asked me to resign and come back to Virginia, where the family could care for my wife. I immediately agreed and told the church deacon committee that I would need to resign immediately.

My wife needed to go back to Virginia as soon as possible, as she was not feeling well. I called my son and asked him to buy a plane ticket for us to fly to Virginia the next day. I stayed in Virginia until June so I could return and preach one last day in Orlando. I gave the sermon on Father's Day to conclude my two years of service there. It was a very emotional good-bye. Everyone was touched by my words of appreciation. While I expected to retire in Orlando, it was not God's will. I really loved them and was reluctant to leave them. It was like the apostle Paul's speech to the elders of Ephesus, as described in Acts chapter 20.

While I was in Orlando, my former church, the Vietnamese Gospel Baptist Church of Alexandria, called me to return as pastor. There had been many pastors since my time in 1987–1995, but God now wanted me to serve them again in July 2010. The church executive committee was treating me so nicely by just having me teach Bible study Saturday night and preaching on Sunday. The Lord was so good to me; he understood the problems in our family as I was caring for my sick wife. He returned me to this former church so I could help the church members increase their knowledge of the Bible.

The executive committee was composed of several ordained ministers and two laymen—good Christians serving the Lord devotedly. The church has been healthy with the Lord's mercy and help. They cooperated closely to solve any church problems and never quarreled. It had obviously grown, and all the members felt good conducting the Lord's work at the church. The sermon CD committee was installed and served by a lady who is a dedicated church member, along with our website technician, who is an ordained minister. The church's website URL is www.vietgospel.org. Two other sites house my sermons as well: www.vietchristian.com and www.tinlanhhyvong.com.

The Vietnamese of the World Hear My Sermons!

Many people around the world e-mailed and called me to say they were interested in my sermons, which were practical, true stories that made the Bible easy to understand. Some listeners I had not met before had such good impressions of my sermons that they sent me physical or monetary gifts. Ministers in Vietnam asked permission to use my sermons with their congregations. I gladly agreed to let them do whatever was good for Christ's work.

A Vietnamese pastor in Australia downloaded my sermons, put them on CDs, and distributed them to people in Vietnam. A Christian from North Vietnam received one and brought it back to play at a wedding banquet. At the end of the sermon, eighty-one banquet attendees accepted the Lord Jesus Christ as their personal Savior. They were gathering to establish a church in North Vietnam. Praise the Lord!

On hearing this news, I was so touched, and I thanked the Lord for using my sermons to save many souls without my presence. I thought it was now time for me to bring the good news of the Lord's salvation around the world for any Vietnamese to take in and trust in the Lord. While I returned to Virginia for my wife's unfortunate illness, the Lord brought me back to broadcast my sermons to the world.

When my wife was well, I would sometimes travel around the world to preach. I was invited to speak in Australia, New Zealand, Germany, France, the Netherlands, Norway, Sweden, Canada, and the United States. I realized, though, that when I traveled I was absent from my church, which caused problems, as my church members still needed to hear my sermons. My current church now loves me because I never miss a Sunday. They are glad for my presence at almost every church meeting. The Lord is allowing his will to be done, and while I am now seventy-five years old, I don't feel the need to retire. My time is used to prepare sermons for the church and the website, which might help people around the world hear God's Word. Before preparing any new sermon, I pray to the Lord for His ideas and teachings, that they might be interesting, meaningful, and helpful for Vietnamese people everywhere.

Although I work hard caring for my wife day and night, I am still healthy enough to prepare the sermons, with the Lord's help. It does not take more than three days to prepare a sermon, and often only one day. I now have the sermons prepared three years in advance, so I can preach a new sermon without preparing anything for three years! Praise the Lord for His grace. I am able to do this in my old age thanks to God's mercy, compassion, and miracles. As Paul said, "I can do all things through Him who strengthens me" (Philippians 4:13).

Chapter 23

My Thanksgiving for God's Miracles

The Bible describes the Pharisees and scribes asking the Lord Jesus Christ to show them a miracle or a sign. Instead, Jesus says, "An evil and adulterous generation craves for a sign; and yet no sign will be given to it but the sign of Jonah the prophet; for just as Jonah was three days and three nights in the belly of the sea monster, so will the Son of Man be three days and three nights in the heart of the earth" (Matthew 12:38–40).

King Herod wanted to meet with Jesus to see the miracles that the people had spoken of. Herod asked Him several questions, but the Lord did not answer. This angered the priests and scribes greatly. He was despised, and they were not pleased that He refused to show them a sign. (See Luke 23:8–11.)

All of these individuals wanted to see a sign or a miracle performed by Jesus because they had heard great things of Him but had not witnessed these things for themselves. The apostle Paul wrote a letter to the Roman church, saying, "For indeed Jews ask for signs and Greeks search for wisdom; but we preach Christ crucified, to Jews a stumbling block and to Gentiles foolishness, but to those who are the called, both Jews and Greeks, Christ the power of God and the wisdom of God" (1 Corinthians 1:22–24).

It is so strange to me that the Jews asked for signs and heard of these signs, and many even saw them, yet people still feared Him and planned to kill Him. The Bible says,

> Therefore, the chief priests and the Pharisees convened a council and were saying, "What are we doing? For this man is performing many signs. If we let Him go on like his, all men will believe in Him, and the Romans will come and take away both our place and our nation." But one of them, Caiaphas, who was high priest that year, said to them, "You know nothing at all, nor do you take into account that it is expedient for you that one man die for the people, and that the whole nation not perish." Now he did not say this on his initiative, but being high priest that year, he prophesied that Jesus was going to die for the nation, and not for the nation only, but in order that He might also gather together into one the children of God who are scattered abroad. So from that day on they planned together to kill Him. (John 11:47–53)

In the Lord Jesus Christ's time, the people who saw His miracles believed in Him because they were the true believers. Those who saw His miracles but made plans to kill Him were not His followers. They were classified as sinners. As Christ said, "But for the cowardly and unbelieving and abominable and murderers and immoral persons and sorcerers and idolaters and all liars, their part will be in the lake that burns with fire and brimstone, which is the second death" (Revelation 21:8).

In the beginning of this book, I spoke of the interesting miracles in the Bible that always interested me as I sat on the first pew of the church, just listening to the sermons about the Lord's life during His earthly ministry. I loved to hear of His miracles because the stories of them described the Lord's works in His will and through His plan to save the ones He loved.

Growing up, I expected to see Him perform His miracles by saving my relatives and people close to me in this life. As I became an adult, though, I experienced much suffering and prayed many times to God for miracles. As I have recorded, I experienced God's miracles on numerous occasions, though sometimes not how I initially expected to experience them. I trusted in the Lord to save me and spread the good news to everyone I met so that we could all together sing praise to Him. Hallelujah; praise the Lord! Allow me to affirm those miracles:

- I was unhealthy, and my mother thought I would die at the age of three, yet I am now seventy-five years old.

- I loved the English language and prayed that I could learn to speak the language and serve God with it.

- I sought education to grow my mind in language and in theology. After many years of education, I earned a doctor of ministry from Liberty Baptist Theological Seminary when I was fifty-nine years old.

- God equipped me for Christian ministry and gave me the strength to serve Him for many years.

- I escaped two bomb explosions while in military service.

- I was discharged and allowed to teach when no one else from the Armed Forces Language School in Saigon had that privilege.

- God sent me visions on two occasions to reassure me and encourage me regarding the journey ahead.

- I was released from imprisonment early and allowed to return to my family.

- My whole family escaped Vietnam on a small wooden boat and made it through storms on the water.

- Forty-seven Vietnamese refugees were rescued at sea.

- Many of the refugees accepted Christ, and their souls were saved through our experience at sea.

- Every time I moved to a new place, I moved according to His will and His plan, as things happened with purpose. God showed me those purposes in His time.

The Lord dwelled in me, spoke to me, encouraged me, comforted me, rebuked me, and taught me. When I would prepare a sermon, he would often wake me from a sound sleep to give me a new idea. He would urge me to go to the computer and add it into the sermon. Sometimes I would change the whole sermon, erasing the old ideas and replacing them with God's new ones. While driving my car, ideas would come to me. I believe these ideas were the ones the Lord wanted me to preach to my congregation.

Section VI
Misunderstanding of God's Miracles

Chapter 24

God Still Performs Miracles

I have heard people say that the miracles God performed in the Bible were intentional and had purpose but were for that phase of the religion. In this modern time, they say, such miracles are no longer effective, given our improvements in science.

No, I don't think so. The book of Acts recorded many miracles, such as when the church was full of the Holy Spirit on the day of Pentecost and the members spoke in foreign languages. Some people said, "They are full of sweet wine" (Acts 2:13). Peter stood up and began speaking: "These men are not drunk" (Acts 2:15). He reminded them of the prophet Joel's words in Joel 2:28–29:

> And it shall be the last days, God says, that I shall pour forth of My Spirit on all mankind; And your sons and your daughters shall prophesy, and your young men shall see visions, and your old men shall dream dreams; Even on My Bond slaves, both men and women, I will in those days pour forth of My Spirit, And they shall prophesy. And I will grant wonders in the sky above and signs on the earth below, blood, and fire, and vapor of smoke. The sun will be turned into darkness and the moon into blood, before the great and glorious day of the Lord shall come. And

it shall be that everyone who calls on the Name of the Lord will be saved. (Acts 2:17–21)

Two thousand years ago, God performed many miracles—even the resurrection of the dead—using many gifted Christians who prayed for the sick. Many miracles happen today to save many people from dangerous circumstances, such as boat rescues, fires, auto accidents, storms, hurricanes, wars, murders, etc. Yes, God's miracles are really still happening and are just as effective as in the Lord Jesus Christ's time.

You might ask why this is. The prophet Joel's prophecy states, "The sun will be turned into darkness and the moon into blood, before the great and glorious day of the Lord shall come. And it shall be that everyone who calls on the Name of the Lord will be saved" (Acts 2:20–21). Are these events miracles of the modern day that will occur before the great and glorious day of the Lord shall come? If you believe that what our dear Lord Jesus Christ prophesied on His return in Matthew chapter 24, Mark 13, and Luke 21 has been fulfilled, then you also believe that God's miracles are still effective.

A Former Pastor's Prophecy on My Future Service to God

Pastor Nguyen, a former director of Mekong River Area Church CMA Association, once met me in Soc Trang Church before the worship service and said to me, "I believe God will still use your English for the near future, Mr. Minh." I consider his words sound, like a prophecy for my future life.

A Strange Recognition

When I left Arkansas for Virginia, a deacon took me to visit a Vietnamese patient in Fairfax Hospital. When he first saw me, he said loudly, "Hi, Pastor!"

I was so surprised and did not know how he knew me, so I asked him, "How did you know I am a pastor?"

He answered, "Nobody told me about you, but some days ago I got a very serious case of pneumonia, and my doctor told my relatives that I might pass away anytime. When I was comatose, I saw you and knew you were my pastor!" I was happy when I heard him say that he met me during his coma. It means that the Lord allowed him to meet with me in his coma, before I even visited him in the hospital, to show that I was selected to be his pastor. I prayed before I left him.

Many Nonbelievers and Believers Accepted the Lord after My Sermons

When I was invited to preach at a church, whether it was my church or a church I was visiting, I often called for an invitation after my sermon. Many people responded to the call by stepping forward and accepting the Lord Jesus Christ as their personal Savior. Many of them became ministers after some years of service as deacons.

Many of the students and church members I taught went on to serve in ministry as deacons, leaders in the church, or ministers.

Dying Taken to Heaven

One thing confirms that God's miracles are still effective, and that is the resurrection of followers of Christ before their death:

- Mr. Tran, a man of seventy years, was sick with stomach cancer. He was brought out of the hospital after being in only one day. I asked him why, and he said, "Last night, I saw heaven, which was so beautiful. I do not like the cancer treatment and would prefer physical death, for an eternal life in heaven." The next day he died peacefully.

- Mrs. Vo, about fifty-five years old, was sick with liver cancer. She was brought home to be cared for by hospice. She told her daughter to ask me not to pray for her, because she saw heaven, full of diamonds, and she would like to die to go there as soon as possible. She died the next day.

- Mr. Nguyen, forty-one years old, was sick with nose cancer. As he lay in the hospital, he accepted the Lord Jesus Christ. The next Saturday, his wife was called to come see him because he was dying. He was dead for eleven minutes but came back to life. I drove to see him the next day, and he told me that on the previous night he had gone to a very beautiful place and met his father, who had died four months prior. When I asked him if he was afraid of death, he said no.

I knew these people and heard them speak of heaven in a way that told me they had seen it. This gave me a strong trust in God's miracles. They guaranteed me that I have been saved and am God's child, who inherits heaven.

My Sermons Are Recorded and Heard Worldwide

My sermons are available at www.vietgospel.org, www.vietchristian.com, and www.tinlanhhyvong.com. Many of my sermons have been watched and heard more than five thousand times. Many Vietnamese e-mail and call to let me know that they have heard my sermons very often and that God taught them through my sermons. My sermons have helped them to grow spiritually in their Christian lives. I am so thankful to the Lord after hearing so. Some people have called me saying that their families became harmonious after hearing my sermons on the subject of family happiness.

I was often invited to pray for the grand openings of businesses like doctor's offices, dentist's offices, barbershops, and nail stores. The owners called me, saying that the Lord has blessed them with prosperity. Praise the Lord for such a blessing! The Lord has blessed my pastorate in making my church grow in both quality and quantity.

Chapter 25

Don't Force God to Perform Miracles

Some people think that God's miracles are available any time, for any prayer. This means that God is ready to heal the patient, save the dead, stop accidents, give the poor money for living, and reunite those separated if there are prayers for those problems. It would seem to me that some people like to force God to perform miracles as a proof of His power and mercy, and to look successful in front of many people.

That, however, is a misunderstanding of God's miracles. God still performs miracles, as I mentioned earlier, because God is love and has mercy and compassion for the suffering. He is not selfish. But that does not mean He does whatever human beings ask for.

The Bible explains it very clearly for us to understand that God performs miracles in His will and for His plan. For instance, Sodom and Gomorrah's destruction by fire and brimstone happened even though Abraham prayed for Lot and his family very earnestly. King Saul asked God for forgiveness of his sins against God twice, but the Spirit went out of him, and he with his three sons died at the battle against the Philistines. The apostle Paul himself wrote that he was taken to the third heaven, and God wanted to keep him from exalting himself by having a messenger of Satan to torment him like a thorn in his flesh. Now read his statement: "Concerning this I implored the Lord three times that it might leave me ... And He has said to me, 'My grace is sufficient for you, for power is perfected in weakness'" (2 Corinthians 12:8–9). What the apostle said means God's answer to him is no.

After returning to Asia Minor on his last mission trip, he stopped by at Miletus and called the elders of the church of Ephesus to him to say a farewell. He said, "And now, behold, bound by the Spirit, I am on my way to Jerusalem, not knowing what will happen to me there, except the Holy Spirit solemnly testifies to me in every city, saying that bonds and afflictions await me. But I do not consider my life of any account as dear to myself, so that I may finish my course and the ministry which I received from the Lord Jesus, to testify solemnly of the gospel of the grace of God" (Acts 20:17–24). He was caught while he was in the temple and taken to Rome for judgment till death.

The Lord Jesus Christ refused to perform miracles for the scribes and the Pharisees, and called them, "an evil and adulterous generation" (Matthew 12:38). He also refused to give signs in front of King Herod, his soldiers, the chief priests, and the scribes. (See Luke 23:8–12.)

God is the Lord, the Creator, "and His name will be called Wonderful Counselor, Mighty God, Eternal Father, Prince of Peace" (Isaiah 9:6b), and "You shall not take the name of the LORD your God in vain, for the LORD will not leave him unpunished who takes His name in vain" (Exodus 20:7). We must be very careful when calling His name for help, not for fun, and not for trying to see whether the miracles happen or not.

God sometimes changed His mind by answering earnest prayers with honesty and integrity. For instance, Hannah prayed to have one son, whom she promised to offer to God as His servant after his birth. God accepted her prayer, and Samuel was born to her family. (See 1 Samuel 1:1–18.) King Hezekiah was about to die, according to Isaiah's statement. The king wept and prayed. The Lord immediately told Isaiah to come back to the palace and tell the king that he would live fifteen more years. (See Isaiah 38:1–8.) Some stories like this demonstrate that the Lord still listens to His children's prayers when they really need His miracles for help. The Lord has blessed my whole life, and God's miracles have demonstrated that He answered my prayers during my sufferings—especially when I fled Vietnam by wooden boat onto the Pacific Ocean and was rescued.

Hallelujah! Praise the Lord Jesus Christ for saving forty-seven Vietnamese refugees on the Pacific Ocean, far from the Vietnamese coastal area. We are so thankful to the ship's captain and Mr. Blaine Buckley for the boat rescue, to the US government, and to Americans for largely opening their arms to receive us in our resettlement. God bless the United States of America. Amen!

Annandale, Virginia

Father's Day, June 15, 2014

God's Miracles in the Bible

Genesis
The creation of the universe and the earth
The creation of the first man and the first woman on the earth
The flood
The creation of the world languages
Abraham's sacrifices and dream
The visit of two angels to Lot; Lot taking his family out of Sodom
Isaac's miraculous birth
Abraham's faith test: a ram caught in the thicket by his horns
The birth of Esau and the birth of Jacob by Isaac's prayers
Jacob's Journey and dream at Bethel
Jacob's wrestling and name change
Joseph's dream
Joseph's becoming the second most important person just after the king
Joseph's discussion of God's plan for his family reunion

Exodus
God's speaking to Moses from the midst of a burning bush that is not consumed
Moses' powers: a miracle with his staff
Aaron's rod becoming a serpent; water being turned to blood
Frogs over the land; the plague of flies

Egyptian cattle dying; the plague of boils; the plague of hail
The plague of locusts; darkness over the land
The last plague
The Passover Lamb; exodus of Israel
God leading the people with a pillar of cloud by day and fire by night
The sea being divided
The Lord providing water
The Lord providing manna; the Lord providing meat
Water in the rock; Amalek fighting
Moses on Sinai; the Ten Commandments
Moses' shining face

Numbers
Miriam becoming leprous for speaking against Moses
The ground swallowing Korah and his families for his rebellion
Fire from the Lord consuming 250 men who were offering incense
Aaron's budding rod; God's selection of Aaron
Moses' striking of the rock twice with his rod; the water of Meribah
The bronze serpent made by Moses
The Lord opening the mouth of the donkey, which talked to Balaam

Deuteronomy
The Lord burying Moses in the valley in the land of Moab

Joshua
Israel crossing the Jordan
The conquest of Jericho
Israel's defeat at Ai; the sin of Achan
Israel's war near Gibeon, in which the sun stood still and the moon stopped.

Judges
Defeat of the army of Sisera
Sign of the fleece
Defeat of the camp of Midian by Gideon's sword
Samson's tearing apart of a young lion
God's splitting of the hollow place so water comes out for Samson to drink
God's strengthening of Samson for him to kill Dagon's worshipers

Ruth
God's enabling of Ruth to give birth to a son, Obed, David's grandfather

1 Samuel
God's enabling of Hannah to give birth to her son Samuel

1 Kings
The gift of flour and oil to a woman's family
The killing of Baal's prophets by God's prophet Elijah
The Lord's presence with the prophet Elijah at Mount Horeb

2 Kings
The prophet Elijah's being taken to heaven with a chariot of fire and horses of fire
The widow's oil; the rising of the Shunammite woman's son; the poisonous stew
Naaman's healing; Gehazi's greed
The axe head's recovery; the blinding of the Arameans
Fulfillment of Elisha's promise
King Hezekiah's illness and recovery

1 Chronicles
Peril in transporting the ark: Uzza's death

Uzziah's undoing as a result of pride

2 Chronicles
Uzziah's infection with leprosy

Job
God's restoration of Job's children and fortunes

Psalms
God's guiding of his children to their desired haven

Isaiah
King Hezekiah's healing

Daniel
The king's forgotten dream; the secret revealed to Daniel
Protection of Daniel's friends
Daniel's interpretation of the handwriting on the wall
Daniel in the lions' den

Jonah
Jonah in the great fish's stomach
The fish's vomiting of Jonah onto the dry land
Jonah's displeasure being rebuked; Jonah seeing the plant become withered

Zechariah
God's commitment to battle Jerusalem's foes

Matthew
Conception and birth of Jesus
The visit of the Magi

Jesus' cleansing of a leper; the centurion's faith; Peter's mother-in-law's healing; Jesus' casting out of demons
A paralytic healed; miracles of healing
A demon-possessed man healed
Five thousand fed
Jesus' walk on the water; four thousand fed; crowds healed
The transfiguration; the demoniac
Sight for the blind
The barren fig tree
Jesus' return from the grave

Mark
Crowds healed
The paralytic healed
Jesus healed on the Sabbath
Jesus' stilling of the sea
The Gerasene demoniac; Jesus' walk on the water
The Syrophoenician woman
Four thousand fed
The transfiguration
Bartimaeus's receipt of sight
The resurrection

Luke
Foretelling of the birth of John the Baptist; foretelling of the birth of Jesus
Jesus' birth in Jerusalem
Many healed
The leper and the paralytic
Jesus' healing of a centurion's servant
Jesus' stilling of the sea; the demoniac cured; miracles of healing
Five thousand fed; the transfiguration
Jesus' healing on the Sabbath

Bartimaeus's receipt of sight
The resurrection
The ascension

John
Miracle at Cana
Healing of a nobleman's son
The healing at Bethesda
Five thousand fed; Jesus' walk on the water
Healing of the man born blind
The death and resurrection of Lazarus
The empty tomb
Jesus' appearance at the Sea of Galilee

Acts
The ascension
The day of Pentecost; filling of the Holy Spirit; languages spoken, three thousand saved and baptized
Healing of the beggar
Fate of Ananias and Sapphira
The conversion of Paul
Peter's arrest and deliverance
Imprisonment of Paul and Silas
Miracles at Ephesus
A conspiracy to kill Paul
Shipwreck

Remarks:

1. The Synoptic Gospels contain the same miracles several times, such as the story of Jesus stilling the sea, which appears in Matthew 8:23–27, Mark 4:35–41, and Luke 8:22–25.

2. The miracles in the book of Revelation are not performed yet and so are not on the list.
3. The apostle Paul performed several miracles that are not detailed. The Bible states that he performed miracles.

Dr. Minh Van Lam's family in Annandale, Virginia—summer 2013.

Dr. and Mrs. Minh Van Lam and their grandchildren in Annandale, Virginia—summer 2013.

CPSIA information can be obtained
at www.ICGtesting.com
Printed in the USA
FFOW04n1021120516
24043FF